# Stress Testing
# the System

# Stress Testing the System

## Simulating the Global Consequences of the Next Financial Crisis

Roger M. Kubarych
Council on Foreign Relations

COUNCIL ON FOREIGN RELATIONS PRESS
NEW YORK

Founded in 1921, the Council on Foreign Relations is a nonpartisan membership organization, research center, and publisher. It is dedicated to increasing America's understanding of the world and contributing ideas to U.S. foreign policy. The Council accomplishes this mainly by promoting constructive discussions and by publishing *Foreign Affairs*, the leading journal on global issues. The Council is host to the widest possible range of views, but an advocate of none, though its research fellows and Independent Task Forces do take policy stands.

From time to time, books, monographs, reports, and papers written by members of the Council's research staff or others are published as a "Council on Foreign Relations Publication."

THE COUNCIL TAKES NO INSTITUTIONAL POSITION ON POLICY ISSUES AND HAS NO AFFILIATION WITH THE U.S. GOVERNMENT. ALL STATEMENTS OF FACT AND EXPRESSIONS OF OPINION CONTAINED IN ALL ITS PUBLICATIONS ARE THE SOLE RESPONSIBILITY OF THE AUTHOR OR AUTHORS.

Council on Foreign Relations books are distributed by Brookings Institution Press (1-800-275-1447). For further information about the Council or this book, please write the Council on Foreign Relations, 58 East 68th Street, New York, NY 10021, or call the Director of Communications at (212) 434-9400. Visit our website at www.cfr.org.

Library of Congress Cataloging-in-Publication Data

Kubarych, Roger M.
    Stress testing the system : simulating the global consequences of the next financial crisis / Roger M. Kubarych.
        p.  cm.
    Includes bibliographical references.
    ISBN 0-87609-271-7
    1. Foreign exchange. 2. International finance. 3. Financial crises. I. Council on Foreign Relations. II. Title.

HG3851 .K817 2001
332'.042—dc21

2001037299

# Contents

# Foreword

A couple of years ago, Council Adjunct Senior Fellow Roger Kubarych and I were musing about the changed state of the world and decided to pursue two related thoughts. One, the obvious one, was that economic and financial matters in many respects had become the heart of international relations and foreign policy. We agreed that we had to explore much further what this obvious point meant. The second idea was to add a different dimension to this process of intellectual exploration—a war game. War-gaming has been a part of policy planning for at least a couple of centuries. Its focus has always been on military threats, however, and it has been built around responding to military scenarios. What Roger and I devised was a war game to be centered essentially around economic and financial crises, with security threats for good measure. Roger took all this and devised a work program for what we called the Financial Vulnerabilities Project, which ultimately led to this book.

The major conclusion that flows from the work of Roger and his colleagues is this: the most dangerous near-term threat to U.S. world leadership and thus to U.S. security, as well, would be a sharp decline in the U.S. securities markets. Such a decline would likely stun the U.S. economy at a time when the strength of our economy is critical to global prosperity, to the financial health and political stability of most nations, and ultimately to international security itself. That is a mouthful, but one with the weight of reality. Let me come back to that point in a moment.

To come to this conclusion, Roger and his Council colleagues conceived and implemented the following series of events:

First, a small roundtable discussion was held involving thirty-five participants, including market practitioners, scholars, and former senior government officials. Participants reviewed lessons learned from recent stock market disturbances and the policy responses to them. They also identified areas of economic and financial vulnerability in the current system and began to describe possible scenarios for how a future market disturbance might unfold.

Second, a brainstorming roundtable was held to develop the fictional scenario detailing political and economic circumstances that formed the backdrop for the policy simulation itself.

Third was a simulation in New York that gathered seventy-five top academics, former policymakers, and Wall Street practitioners to work through the options and constraints facing the U.S. government in the aftermath of a sudden and significant stock market decline.

Fourth, a conference was held in New York for a broad audience of both Council members and selected invitees to disseminate the findings of the roundtable and the policy simulation.

Fifth was a second simulation for Council members in Chicago.

Sixth, a conference was held in Washington, D.C., to disseminate findings from the project and discuss financial vulnerabilities in the current system with a policy-oriented audience.

Seventh, Roger toured through Texas and California to share the findings of the simulation and to promote the use of simulations as a means to prepare for an unexpected downturn in the financial markets.

As the array of very experienced people went through these steps, they returned again and again to the underlying reality of the power of the U.S. securities market. As I observed the "war game" as it unfolded, it seemed to me that the operating principle of the decision-makers was that their first duty was to stabilize markets. As long as they kept the markets stable, they reasoned, other problems could be made manageable; and if the markets tumbled out of control, all other problems would become less manageable and more dangerous. That is the ultimate lesson derived from the Kubarych project and this book. Roger and his colleagues believe that conscientious government policy-makers have to dedicate the time and the resources necessary to identify key vulnerabilities in the international economic system in order to prepare for the consequences of crises in advance.

Allow me a brief word of caution here. War games are not meant to predict, and the Council on Foreign Relations certainly is not predicting economic upturns or downturns. War games are intended to help the people who will make decisions learn how to think about those decisions in advance.

Roger Kubarych is a colleague anybody in the idea business would want to have. He knows a tremendous amount and is open-minded; he loves to engage and is incredibly creative.

Council Chairman Peter G. Peterson and Vice Chair Maurice R. Greenberg join me in congratulating Roger and his colleagues (whom he justly thanks in his acknowledgments) for this fine enterprise and book.


*Leslie H. Gelb*
President
Council on Foreign Relations

# Acknowledgments

This book is the outcome of an ambitious project on the broad policy implications of vulnerabilities in the global economic and financial system. The Financial Vulnerabilities Project was initiated in the fall of 1999, shortly after I joined the Council on Foreign Relations after many years working on Wall Street. Since then, the project has spawned a score of meetings and conferences, involving the intensive collaboration of dozens of Council members and staff and the active involvement of hundreds more. The centerpiece of the project was a scenario-based simulation held here at the Council in New York on January 22, 2000, at which seventy-five distinguished experts in the fields of monetary policy, financial regulation, economic and trade policy, foreign relations, and national security grappled with more than two dozen fictional policy problems cutting across all of these disciplines. Over a pressure-packed eight hours, they were challenged to identify the policy options and constraints that would face the U.S. government in the aftermath of a severe (though explicitly hypothetical) global financial disturbance. This book is essentially an amalgamation and distillation of their collective energy, imagination, and commitment, and I am grateful for the contribution of each participant. A complete list of participants can be found in the appendixes.

I would like to offer special thanks to a number of individuals who provided vital support and guidance.

First is Les Gelb, president of the Council on Foreign Relations, who came up with the idea of the simulation in the first place. He asked: Why not construct a kind of "war game" to work through the impact of the next financial crisis, not only on the global economy and the markets, but also on foreign policy and national security? I went off to assess the feasibility of doing just that. When I assured him we could do it, but it would be a prodigious undertaking, he was unsparing in providing the resources required to organize and successfully run such a complex exercise.

Second is Henry Kaufman, president of Henry Kaufman & Company, Inc., my long-time business associate and mentor. His generosity took many forms, not least providing the intellectual framework for visualizing how economic and financial events affect the global system. Henry has long insisted that in making predictions about future economic and financial prospects we must not merely extrapolate from the past but we must "look around the corner." He has taught that it is only by seeking to anticipate unconventional—and occasionally unprecedented— developments and assess their impact that investors and policy- makers can make wise decisions. That message animated our whole effort.

Third is John J. Phelan, former chair of the New York Stock Exchange, under whom I served as chief economist in those fateful days of October 1987 when the markets were roiled by one of the most spectacular convulsions in history. His calm and decisive leadership at the time, especially his ability to sense what needed to be done to restore confidence in the markets, sets a high standard for current and future officials. He also has an encyclopedic memory of other, less theatrical shocks to the markets, on which we drew heavily in developing the project.

At many points along the way, the contributions of Council on Foreign Relations colleagues were pivotal. Central to the suc- cess of the January 2000 simulation was the written scenario that laid out the fictional context for the policy problems that would engage participants. Countless hours were spent drafting and editing the scenario to inject just the right mixture of plausibility and challenge. Virtually the entire Studies Department, headed by Lawrence Korb, assisted in this task. Likewise, organizing the logistics of the simulation and running the various meetings and conferences that were integral to the project required tireless efforts on the part of many. I am particularly grateful to Military Fellow and U.S. Navy Capt. David A. Duffié, Visiting Fellow for Intelligence Paul Heer, Charlie Day, Leigh Gusts, David Kellogg, Anne Luzzatto, Walter Russell Mead, Michael Peters, Gideon Rose, Jacqui Schein, Marcia Sprules, Benn Steil, and Bruce Stokes, all of whom helped to bring the project to life. In addition, another two dozen Council research associates and other staff members provided invaluable assistance. No one was more instrumental in making the right things happen at the right time, however, than my gifted research associate during 1999–2000, Céline Gustavson. She oversaw every last detail of the simulation planning and helped administer the numerous meetings that led up to the simulation and followed it, especially the highly successful July 2000 conference "The Next Financial Crisis: Warning Signs, Damage Control, and Impact."

With regard to the simulation itself, I would like to acknowledge the indispensable contributions of leaders Robert Carswell, Amb. William Clark, Richard Goeltz, John Heimann, and Amb. Jim Jones, as well as roving journalists Andrew Hilton and David Shirreff. Without their enthusiasm and ingenuity, the whole exercise could have fallen flat and certainly would not have achieved the remarkable degree of success all the participants helped create. Special thanks should also go to Kenneth W. Dam, Michael H. Moskow, John E. Rielly, and David Coolidge for helping me conduct an abbreviated simulation in September 2000 at the Chicago Council on Foreign Relations. I am also particularly grateful to Paula Dobriansky and Amy Drapeau for organizing a conference for Council members in Washington, D.C., in December 2000; to Irina Faskianos for arranging my sessions with Council members in Dallas, Houston, Los Angeles, and San Francisco in January 2001; and to Scott Pardee for inviting me to preview the simulation findings for students and faculty of Middlebury College in March 2001.

Many individuals involved in the simulation offered valuable feedback on the manuscript. I especially appreciate the time these people took to read drafts, write helpful comments, and point me in the right direction when I steered off track. Nicholas F. Beim, Deborah K. Burand, Sam Y. Cross, Jack David, Hans Decker, Jessica P. Einhorn, George J.W. Goodman, David Gordon, Marc Levinson, Martin Mayer, Cynthia A. Tindell, and Melvin F. Williams critiqued drafts of the manuscript, while Craig Drill, Adm. William (Bud) Flanagan, and Martin Gross gave valuable insights on the book's conclusions.

Finally, I would like to acknowledge the intelligence, persistence, and dedication of my present research associate, Laura Winthrop, who has painstakingly edited several drafts of the manuscript for this book. On behalf of all potential readers, she has been relentless in urging me to tighten every paragraph, clarify every assertion, and substantiate every conclusion. We are all in her debt.

*Roger M. Kubarych*
Henry Kaufman Adjunct Senior Fellow
for International Economics and Finance
Council on Foreign Relations

# An Introduction

*Washington policymakers are suddenly confronted by a raft of economic and financial problems stemming from an outbreak of severe turbulence in U.S. and other world stock markets. Compounding the mess are a number of delicate foreign policy issues, some with potentially damaging consequences for U.S. national security.*

*In Mexico, controversy over irregularities in the recent presidential election has led to sporadic violence and a surge of illegal immigration to the United States. In Brazil, financial conditions have dramatically worsened. The Brazilian authorities are unable to make normal payments on the country's large outstanding debt and are considering options that could discriminate against U.S. creditors. In the Middle East, Saudi Arabia is weighing closer ties with Iran and even with Iraq, in defiance of long-standing U.S. policies. In Turkey, a banking crisis looms, while on Capitol Hill, critics of alleged Turkish human rights abuses are pressing for American sanctions on military shipments to that country. Meanwhile, intelligence sources warn that material that might be used to produce a nuclear weapon has been stolen from Russian storehouses and is reported to have been shipped to Libya.*

These are some of the hypothetical scenarios we put to nearly seventy-five distinguished experts in the fields of monetary policy, financial regulation, economics and trade policy, foreign policy, and national security. These experts came to the Council on Foreign Relations in New York on January 22, 2000, ready to participate in a scenario-based policy simulation. They were given the same sort of mandate that policymakers typically set for their advisers: prepare recommendations for dealing with difficult policy problems. In the simulation, all the plot lines and policy problems were hypothetical, though some drew on actual antecedents. However, the experience of dealing with rapidly unfolding events that create complex policy dilemmas was genuinely true to life.

This book lets you "listen in" on the deliberations of this group of experts in two broad policy areas: first, how to develop appropriate monetary and fiscal policies to deal with a global economic and financial crisis, and second, how to address foreign policy and national security challenges in a number of countries and regions around the world. You will learn what problems received highest priority, what policy remedies were considered, which alternatives were rejected, which were supported, and how the experts came to their decisions. The book also provides a broader real-world context: it is essential in the post–Cold War world to develop new ways of thinking about foreign policy and national security given that they are increasingly and inextricably linked with economics and markets.

# Chapter I

# Economics and Finance at Center Stage

The world has changed since the end of the Cold War in a host of ways. But perhaps the most significant and probably most durable change is that economics and financial markets have taken center stage in how foreign policy and national security is perceived and managed. The specific shocks that have produced the extraordinary problems of recent years—ranging from Mexico in 1994–95, Asia in 1997–98, Russia and Brazil later that year, and Argentina and Turkey in 2000–2001—have not been solely economic or financial in character. Instead, those episodes have put into play all aspects of U.S. relations with the affected countries or regions. They have also exposed occasionally sharp differences with our allies, with regard to both assessment and prescription. Thus, the U.S. government has had to forge policy responses out of imperfect information and divergent analyses of what has gone wrong and how to repair it. A number of experts have criticized policy officials for being unprepared to anticipate these events and mitigate their adverse consequences. Several have saved their harshest criticism for the level of preparedness of multilateral institutions such as the International Monetary Fund (IMF), the World Bank, or in some cases the United Nations.[1] But hardly anyone in the markets or in academia

1

can boast of having accurately foreseen the breadth and depth of the economic and financial problems, or their broader political dimensions.

Policymaking is not going to get any easier in the coming years. The management of the kinds of financial, economic, and political flare-ups that governments are likely to face in the future will require new perspectives and upgraded technical skills because the issues increasingly cut across traditional intellectual and policy disciplines.

The purpose of the policy simulation that was held at the Council on Foreign Relations on January 22, 2000, was to conduct an exercise that could help policymakers and their advisers become better prepared for the challenges associated with a rapidly changing and increasingly complex international environment. We, as the planners of the simulation, sought to confront participants with difficult hypothetical policy problems that would test their expertise and judgment. We also wanted to get them to think across accustomed lines and to consider policy responses outside the confines of their own specific disciplines. Most would agree that interdisciplinary approaches to problem solving make sense in theory. But in practice, coaxing experts to reach out to and perhaps defer to specialists in other fields is a tough undertaking, even within an explicitly fictional scenario-based simulation.

Simulations often make it easier to think unconventionally. Employing scenarios, because they are forward-looking and works of fiction (but naturally based on our knowledge of the markets), encourages and allows people to use their imaginations in an environment unconstrained by the inhibitions of widely accepted analyses. On difficult problems, many options are ruled out because policymakers face constraints imposed by what are familiarly described as "conditions on the ground." Scenario-based simulations permit participants to relax assumptions and let in unorthodox options that would normally be dismissed in the real world. Further, simulations can level hierarchy in bureaucratic organizations, whether in the public or private sector, and permit interchanges that might have been uncomfortable under normal conditions. In the real world, subordinates often find it difficult, and at times career threatening, to confront their superiors with the possibility that their assumptions about the future might be faulty. By contrast, the theater of a simulation allows a franker discussion than might be possible in more traditional and more structured meetings.

## Antecedents: Military, Business, Financial

Scenario-based simulations are an ancient tradition. The classic scenario-based simulation is the "war game." The Swedish Defense Wargaming Centre, an international authority on the history of war games, remarks that: "the first military commanders tried to visualize the most conceivable course of events with the help of small stones and simple wooden models. The early forms of chess in ancient China and India (500 B.C.) represent the first known exemplification of modeling and simulation of war, in other words a kind of war game."[2]

Fast forward to a curious example of the use of war-gaming in the seventeenth century. It revolves around the saga of an obscure Scotsman, Patrick Gordon. This soldier of fortune was elevated by Czar Peter the Great of Russia to be his chief military counselor in 1694. Among his diverse talents, Gordon conducted the war-game maneuvers of Peter's specially trained troops.[3]

According to Matthew Caffrey, professor of war-gaming and campaign planning at the College of Aerospace Doctrine Research and Education (CADRE), modern war-gaming originated with a father-son combination of the Reisswitz family in Prussia in the early nineteenth century. In 1811, the elder Herr von Reisswitz, who was the Prussian war counselor at Breslau, invented a war game that went beyond earlier chess-based methods. Dispensing with the traditional "chess board," he constructed a sand table that modeled actual terrain. He represented units by blocks that were in the scale of the terrain, representing regiments in columns. In the game, Caffrey notes, "each player would give orders to an umpire who was required to update the terrain table, resolve combat, and tell the players only what they would know at that point in an actual situation. To determine casualties, umpires first consulted complex tables that indicated likely attrition based on range, terrain, and other factors. The exact attrition was determined by a roll of dice, which depicted the uncertainties of the battlefield!"[4]

Later Reisswitz's son adapted his father's invention and made it more practical for an army on the move by dispensing with sand tables and replacing them with topographic maps. In 1824, the young Lieutenant Reisswitz demonstrated his innovation to the Prussian Chief of Staff, Gen. Karl von Muffling, who excitedly proclaimed, "It's not a game at all, it's training for war. I shall recommend it enthusiastically to the whole army."[5]

Military wargaming continued to evolve over the coming decades but truly came into its own in the period between World War I and World War II. The renowned American seaman Fleet Adm. Chester A. Nimitz, in reflecting on the war games he played and supervised during the 1930s, commented that "the war with Japan had been reenacted in game rooms at the War College by so many people, and in so many ways, that nothing that happened during the war was a surprise—absolutely nothing, except the Kamikaze tactics toward the end of the war. We had not visualized these."[6]

Perhaps the most effective use of scenario-based military simulations took place in the headquarters of the German army in the years 1939 and 1940. This is the verdict of Harvard historian Ernest R. May, who recently published the definitive book on Germany's successful May 1940 invasion of France, entitled *Strange Victory: Hitler's Conquest of France*. According to May, "Though most armies used war games, the German army took them more seriously than most."[7] In December 1939, pressed by Hitler to finish plans for an invasion of France, Gen. Franz Halder, German army chief of staff, ordered a day-long war game to test three possible versions of the offensive attack through the Low Countries, code-named "Plan Yellow."[8] In the strategic simulation of Plan Yellow, respected German intelligence officers played the roles of key French and British commanders. The part of Gen. Maurice Gamelin, France's chief of staff of national defense and the commander of Allied forces, was played by the decorated World War I veteran, Army Intelligence Col. Ulrich Liss.

In the simulation, "Liss did not have to act according to German principles, but was supposed to adopt decisions and measures which . . . the Allied command would presumably have followed."[9] Liss's incisive analysis of Gamelin and the military-political milieu in which he worked led him to conclude that the French and their British allies would be expecting the spearhead of the German assault to come through Belgium and the Netherlands. As May puts it "On game tables and in memoranda, [Liss] and his colleagues assured the generals that French and British forces would rush into Belgium, that the Allied high command would leave weak forces behind to cover the Ardennes, and that, once they grasped what was going on, they would still be slow to redirect their efforts toward the true German *Schwerpunkt.*"[10] The furious blitzkrieg through the Ardennes forest that sealed the German victory over France and Britain in May 1940 proceeded almost exactly as participants in the simulation had envisaged.

May argues that Liss's accurate portrayal of the Allied commander as a fallible person, and not an idealized model, probably contributed to the acceptance and eventual implementation of a plan that had initially been discarded as too risky. May concludes, "As far as I know, no intelligence analyst has ever, in all of human history, had comparable influence on a great event."[11]

Scenario-based simulations are relatively recent additions to the tools of strategic planning used by business corporations. But they have proved to be increasingly useful, especially in the field of risk management. A number of businesses, government agencies, and think tanks have had notable results using scenario-based simulations to get people to think about seemingly unlikely but potentially costly events. One of the earliest successes was by Royal Dutch/Shell in the 1980s just as oil prices were peaking.[12] The company's strategy staff, led by Pierre Wack, challenged senior executives' conventional projections by simulating the effects of a hypothesized big drop in the price of oil at a time when almost every oil market expert, scholar, politician, and journalist saw prices going up inexorably. Forced to think through the consequences of an unlikely, but plausible, scenario, Shell managers did not make perfect decisions, but they navigated the eventual collapse in oil prices in 1985–86 better than those companies that did not have in place such a systematic method of stress testing.

More recently, financial institutions, including large banks, securities firms, and insurance companies, have been using complex computer models to evaluate the sensitivity of their assets and liabilities to sharp fluctuations in asset prices, interest rates, and foreign currency rates. They have sought to estimate with some precision the value at risk in their businesses, investment portfolios, and joint ventures. These model-based risk assessment systems are a definite improvement on more impressionistic methods used in years past. But they are still essentially backward-looking, since they are based on statistical formulas estimated using past data. They help in preparing only for events that resemble those of the past. Simulations, by contrast, allow for a much greater range of possibilities to be considered, including developments without historical precedent. That is why the institutions that have achieved the greatest success in identifying and managing risk have done so by supplementing their computer models with scenario-based simulations.

## Guiding Principles for Constructing the Scenario

Most scenarios that have been conducted outside the military have focused on a single event, such as Shell Oil's simulation of a possible oil price drop. Similarly, financially oriented exercises have been centered upon a specific financial mishap. A remarkably effective case of this type of work is the simulation organized by the London-based Centre for the Study of Financial Innovation, entitled *The Fall of Mulhouse Brand.*[13] By stimulating an in-depth examination of one route by which a financial institution might collapse, it was a truly fascinating exercise with profound implications for financial regulatory policy. But its technical sophistication keeps "Mulhouse Brand" from having broader relevance for policymakers in disciplines other than financial supervision and regulation.

In our simulation, we decided to go in a different direction. We sought to construct an exercise that put the emphasis on *complexity* and *time pressure*. In order to achieve this, we piled on a multiplicity of policy problems, intentionally more numerous than the participants could reasonably be expected to handle in the allotted time (eight hours at the New York simulation on January 22, 2000, and two hours in the abbreviated version in Chicago on September 26, 2000). We wanted the players to have to exercise policy triage, that is, to consciously prioritize policy problems—to choose which to deal with in depth, which to treat with cursory attention, and which to pass over entirely.

We also intended for the simulation to have a genuinely global perspective. The aim was to get participants to explore the ramifications of a financial convulsion that had origins in the United States but would soon envelop all major financial markets and all regions of the world. The novel element was the explicit recognition of potential foreign policy and national security considerations that flowed, directly or indirectly, from financial and economic causes.

Moreover, in constructing the background scenario, we wanted to go far beyond equities markets. To demonstrate the linkages among markets and countries, we constructed our scenario to have repercussions on bond markets, currency markets, and commodity markets. That is, interest rates, exchange rates, and key commodity prices, especially oil, would display the same heightened volatility as stock prices. From the outset and throughout, participants would have no clear guide as to whether there was any safe haven from our fictional financial squall.

This represented a sharp departure from the actual circumstances in the second half of the 1990s. The last significant financial crisis—the Asian debt crisis of 1997–98 that eventually spread to Russia and then Brazil—turned out to be, on balance, favorable for the United States. In that sequence of shocks, America's financial markets were genuinely the safe haven for investors from all around the world seeking to protect their wealth. The United States certainly could boast of favorable economic fundamentals at the time. It was virtually alone in generating a strong economy, low inflation, a roaring stock market, credible monetary policy, and a stable political configuration that was producing a remarkable budget surplus. Admittedly, there were longer-term concerns about the low savings rate on the part of American households and the sizable buildup of debt both by households and by corporations. The heavy private-sector borrowing supported spending in excess of the production of the U.S. economy, which showed up in large merchandise trade and current-account deficits with the rest of the world. But to global investors fearful of incurring large losses on their investments in Asia, Latin America, or Eastern Europe, the U.S. financial markets appeared to be insulated against financial contagion for some time to come.

In short, by the beginning of 2000, in the real world of New York, London, and Tokyo, not to mention Washington, few were worrying about the next financial crisis and, among those who were, most more or less took for granted that the United States would not be in danger even in the unlikely event of another major financial crisis.

Our scenario, if it was going to force the simulation participants to think about the unthinkable, had to be based on plot lines that would effectively raise doubts about each one of the perceived elements of strength in the U.S. position. Internally, we thought of the scenario as posing a "threat to American triumphalism."

That logically entailed a number of building blocks.

First, we felt that the motivating factor had to be a shock to the American stock market. Nobody knows what causes stock market crashes. But we all know from history that they do happen. They usually happen at a time when the overwhelming majority of ordinary investors are bullish and when the bulk of press coverage of the markets is bullish, too. These were the circumstances of late 1999–early 2000: electrifying initial public offerings (IPOs) that captured the imagination and the money of thousands of investors; large numbers of mergers and acquisitions that both puzzled and dazzled experts and amateur investors alike; and breathless TV commentators interviewing the latest high-flying stock picker. Since the high-tech bubble was at the heart of the stock market advance, we felt it was important to launch the scenario with a hypothetical development that would call into question the infatuation with high-tech companies. We chose to suppose a sharp falloff in sales of new computers as businesses decided that they had done enough procurement during the run-up to Y2K, with across-the-enterprise software upgrades to enable computer programs to function properly after January 1, 2000.*

Once we had the U.S. stock market in descent, we had the raw material for a situation in which latent resentment toward real or imagined American hubris and arrogance, in no small measure spawned and justified by Wall Street's long bull market run, could burst out in various ways. We intended to build plot lines into the simulation that had several countries or groupings of countries go out of their way to challenge U.S. views on and interests in economic, financial, and international matters.

In putting our scenario together, we realized that too severe a financial shock would make such a challenge implausible. In this case, foreign markets and businesses alike would be so terrified of a global recession they would look to U.S. leadership to

---

* Y2K was the name for the massive effort to reprogram computer software so that it could handle data for the new century; in order to conserve expensive and intially limited data-storage capacity, software was originally written with just the last two digits of the year, presumably on the expectation that it would be replaced by whole new versions. But companies continued to use the old software, improving it as they went along. Hence the need for the multibillion-dollar effort that spawned not only fixes for Y2K but widespread upgrades. The trouble was that to run the new software, businesses had to purchase new, bigger, faster, and more powerful computers.

get the world out of it. Likewise, foreign governments would tend to defer to U.S. policy judgments. So for the simulation to be a worthwhile exercise, the hypothesized financial shock, while serious, could not be catastrophic. Detailed data on market developments communicated to participants throughout the simulation were crafted with this constraint in mind.

Second, we had to start out with the premise that the most straightforward and universally recommended policy response during past financial shocks—an easing of monetary policy by the Federal Reserve—would not in itself be sufficient to solve the market problem. If aggressive monetary easing was all it took to restore stability in the markets and produced no adverse side effects on inflation, there would be no dilemma and hence no difficult problem for simulation participants to try to resolve. So we visualized a set of conditions that would inhibit, at least for some part of the simulation, an unconstrained effort by our Central Banking Group to stabilize the markets through monetary accommodation. One inhibitor was to hypothesize a sudden, sharp rise in the U.S. inflation rate. Another inhibitor was to put the dollar under downward pressure in the foreign exchange markets.*

Third, we had to allow other countries to become uncooperative with the United States, even when a fully logical, dispassionate assessment would have concluded that their own interests would be best pursued through policy coordination. But from the perspective of other countries, a reasonably contained market correction for U.S. financial markets might not have been viewed as an entirely bad thing. For Europeans, it would have meant at least a respite from the progressive weakening in the value of the euro during 1998–99, which had been a source of considerable disappointment to the advocates of a European common currency and an aggravation for European inflation. For the

* Note that at least one astute participant thought a stronger dollar was the more realistic consequence of the global disturbance and that a rise in the dollar's value would have created even harder policy problems. The only way to tell if that is true would be to run the simulation over again with the altered assumption!

Japanese, it would have shifted the spotlight away from the country's nagging economic and financial problems and eased Japan's regional relationships. For emerging economies, it would have opened up some opportunities for charting a more independent course, whether in terms of managing problems or exploring economic, financial, or political opportunities.

Appendix A contains the full text of the written scenario, entitled "The Story So Far . . . ," which was sent to all participants in advance of the simulation on January 22, 2000. The scenario laid out the hypothetical events that had transpired in the weeks and months leading up to the simulation. When participants arrived to play the game, they received additional background information and were told what policy problems they would be called upon to resolve.

## Organization of the Simulation

Although we decided early in the planning process that we would try to emulate conditions in the real world of policy-making as closely as possible, we realized that it would be necessary to simplify for the purpose of the game. With this in mind, we designed a simulation to challenge the analytical and policy-making skills of some seventy-five individuals with considerable expertise in international relations, the economy, and finance. They included current and former public officials, business executives, financial market practitioners, lawyers, economists, and scholars. They came on a Saturday in January 2000 prepared to spend eight hours wrestling with upwards of twenty-five complex policy problems involving more than thirty countries from almost all parts of the globe. Their only background reading was the scenario, neutrally titled "The Story So Far . . . ," which described the origins of the fictional financial disturbance and hinted at the wide array of financial, economic, foreign policy, and even national security repercussions that would ensue. The participants were divided into five groups:

1. The Decision-Makers Group, representing senior White House and cabinet officials and the congressional leadership;

2. The Central Banking Group, representing the Federal Reserve System;

3. The Financial Regulatory Group, representing agencies such as the Securities and Exchange Commission (SEC), the Commodity Futures Trading Commission (CFTC), and the Federal Deposit Insurance Commission (FDIC);

4. The Economics and Trade Group, representing the policy planners of the Treasury Department and the office of the U.S. Trade Representative;

5. The Foreign Policy and National Security Group, representing the Departments of State and Defense.

Within this multilayered structure, we assigned specific roles to individual participants in the executive branch and included members of Congress in order to more closely parallel the structure that surrounds real-life political decision-making.* However, we purposely did not have anyone play the president himself, because we wanted to focus on developing policy recommendations rather than presidential decisions.

Why such a complicated organizational structure? The reason is that governmental decision-making in the United States is genuinely untidy. Each administration has vast powers but is confined by the system of checks and balances. In the financial arena, authority is especially diffuse, which further complicates decision-making in this area.

To begin with, the Federal Reserve, as an independent central bank, has virtual autonomy in domestic monetary policy formulation and is subject only to congressional approval. When the Fed—or, in our simulation, the Central Banking Group—formulates monetary policy, it normally informs top Treasury and

---

* See Appendix D for the designations, as well as the full list of participants in the simulation.

White House officials of its decisions, but it does not ask permission to proceed. It does not even have a mandate to consult with them.* But the Fed is explicitly subordinate to the U.S. Treasury with regard to policy toward the foreign exchange value of the dollar, notwithstanding the importance of foreign exchange rate movements for the U.S. economy and the financial markets— and thus indirectly for domestic monetary policy.** This dichotomy was faithfully replicated in our simulation.

The structure for supervising and regulating financial institutions in the United States is similarly convoluted. Authority over the banking system is split among the Federal Reserve, the Office of the Comptroller of the Currency (OCC), the FDIC, and fifty state banking commissioners. The securities industry is regulated by the SEC, an independent regulatory agency, in conjunction with various state securities regulators. But operationally the SEC delegates considerable regulatory authority to self-regulatory institutions, prominently the New York Stock Exchange (NYSE) and the National Association of Securities Dealers (NASD). The regulatory departments of both institutions are heavily staffed by SEC alumni. However, though it seems complex, even this demarcation is oversimplified. Ever since the Glass-Steagall Act was repealed in 1999, bank holding companies can own and operate broker-dealers, and as a result, both the Fed and the SEC are involved in their supervision and regulation. In addition, there is an FDIC-like entity that insures the accounts of individual investors with their brokers—the little known, but potentially critical, Securities Industry Protection Corporation (SIPC).***

Similar regulatory overlap is present in other areas of the institutional architecture of finance. For example, professional

* Jawboning, or more public forms of pressure, by the administration on the Fed has occurred in the past; however, the Clinton-Rubin-Summers team largely left the Greenspan-led central bank on its own. Early signs are that the new Bush administration is following that route, too.
** The Fed is not commonly shy about presenting its views on the dollar to the Treasury; while this discussion is normally conducted internally, it occasionally spills over to the public.
*** In the simulation, the financial regulatory expert group was forced to consider problems with electronic brokerages that raised tough questions about the financial health of the SIPC.

investment advisers are registered by the SEC, subject to rules of pension fund management set up by the Department of Labor, and are also subject to lawsuits from clients who feel they have breached their fiduciary duty.*

The area of financial derivatives provides another illustration of regulatory complexity and confusion.** The CFTC, yet another independent agency, has the mandate to regulate exchange-traded commodities futures, including financial futures and futures on options, but it is not authorized to regulate the same sort of derivatives contracts that are struck outside the exchanges, i.e., over-the-counter futures, options, and swaps.

When it comes to the huge insurance industry, there is no regulator at the federal level whatsoever—all supervision is conducted at the state level by state insurance commissioners. Finally, some segments of the U.S. financial system, responsible for a large percentage of credit creation and trading activity in the markets, have no regulator. Hedge funds are a highly publicized example, but thousands of mortgage banks and finance companies are also largely or even entirely unregulated.

In the scenario, many of the difficult hypothetical financial problems that simulation participants had to grapple with turned on uncertainty about which regulator should be responsible for the troubled institutions that do not fit neatly into familiar categories.

The final element of the organizational structure of the simulation is the role of what we called the Control Room. This group was made up of eight staff members who essentially controlled the game and revealed to participants, in email updates every fifteen minutes, how the international financial crisis was unfolding. The Control Room sent out news bulletins to each of the groups with regular updates on what the markets were doing. It relayed intelligence briefings, reports on foreign government

---

* This element was a central ingredient in "The Story So Far . . . ."
** Financial derivatives are financial instruments that have no intrinsic value on their own but derive their value from something else such as common stocks, bonds, foreign currencies, or commodities. The most commonly used are forwards, futures, swaps, and options.

actions, news of international disasters, and a host of un-confirmed rumors. It answered questions from expert group participants on a myriad of matters, "factual" questions on the condition of troubled financial institutions, and policy-related questions on what foreign officials were planning to say or do.

In designing the simulation, we made the decision that it would be beyond our capabilities to set up individual teams to represent each of the foreign governments and central banks that presented policy problems for the United States. But we anticipated that participants would want to be able to interact and negotiate with the representatives of foreign governments, so we had the Control Room play the role of the "rest of the world." Depending on the circumstances, the Control Room conveyed the perspective of the Group of Seven (G-7) leading industrialized nations, the European Central Bank (ECB), or the IMF, to name a few.[14] The Control Room also played the role of specific foreign officials—though it must be said, not always with the complete admiration of certain participants who felt that the role-playing was not entirely accurate given their personal experience with these officials in real life. They may well have been right, but after all, the whole scenario was intended as a work of fiction!

## Notes

1.  See, for instance, U.S. Congress. Senate. Committee on Foreign Relations. "The Meltzer Commission: The Future of the IMF and World Bank: Hearing before the Committee on Foreign Relations," U.S. Senate, 106th Congress, 2nd session, May 23, 2000; Jeffrey Sachs, "Out of the Frying Pan into the IMF Fire," *The Observer,* February 8, 1998, 5.

2.  Swedish Defense Wargaming Centre, "The History of War-games." http://www.fksc.mil.se/hist/histe.html.

3.  Britannica.com, "Gordon, Patrick."

4.  Lt. Col. Matthew Caffrey Jr. (USAF-Ret.), "Toward a History-Based Doctrine for Wargaming," *Aerospace Power Journal* 14, No. 2 (fall 2000): 34–5.

_16    Stress Testing the System_

5.  Ibid., 35.

6.  William B. Scott, "Wargames Revival Breaks New Ground," _Aviation Week and Space Technology_, November 2, 1998, 56.

7.  Ernest R. May, _Strange Victory: Hitler's Conquest of France_ (New York: Hill and Wang, 2000), 257–8.

8.  Ibid., 227.

9.  Franz Halder, "Grundlagen für die Lage Rot," December 15, 1939, NARS Film T 78, Reel 454; cited in May, _Strange Victory_, 259.

10. May, _Strange Victory_, 268.

11. Ibid.

12. Peter Schwartz, _The Art of the Long View_ (New York: Doubleday, 1991), 7.

13. David Shirreff and David Lascelles, _The Fall of Mulhouse Brand_ (London: The Centre for the Study of Financial Innovation, 1997).

14. The G-7, which includes the United States, Canada, Japan, the United Kingdom, Germany, France, and Italy, is the core group for the annual economic summit that brings heads of government together to discuss economic and financial issues, as well as broader security matters on occasion.

# Chapter II

# Stabilizing the
# Financial Markets:
# The Focal Point
# of the Simulation

## Preparing the Scenario

The organizing principle behind the simulation was that the fictional financial disturbance would have far-reaching effects on global financial conditions, the world economy, and broader foreign policy and security relations. However, we felt it would be a mistake to concoct a scenario that mirrored past crises too closely.

Take, for instance, the October 1987 stock market break. Something of the speed and magnitude of that convulsion, in which the Dow Jones industrial average plunged 25 percent in a single day, would naturally command the undivided attention of every department of government and push aside everything else, especially seemingly unrelated foreign policy events. Instead of having a similarly huge crisis unfold during the simulation, our scenario began with much of the initial damage to the financial markets already done. During the simulation itself, the second- and third-round impacts of the fictional financial crisis were designed to unfold in bits and pieces, leaving the global financial system in perilous condition but not without incipient signs that markets were bottoming out. Future events were purposely left ambiguous so that simulation participants would have to reach their own judgments on how vulnerable the markets were to new pressures.

The Asian financial crisis of 1997–98 was not a relevant precedent, either, simply because of the fact that the United States largely benefited from that emergency. As frightened global investors looked for a safe haven, huge amounts of capital were diverted into U.S. financial markets and into the dollar. That helped drive down U.S. interest rates, while the strong dollar exchange rate lowered import costs and thus held back American inflation. By contrast, our scenario was designed to stress test conventional wisdom—which held that the United States, the sole superpower in military terms, was also the preeminent economic and financial power, with the strength and resiliency to shrug off any and all traumas. A scenario that revolved around the notion of a "challenge to American triumphalism" had to position the United States as a victim, not a beneficiary.

Anyone who has ever tried to identify downside risks, whether to a company, an investment portfolio, or a government policy, would concede that it is futile to claim an analyst can know ahead of time precisely how a financial, or any other type of crisis, will unfold. But when constructing a credible scenario, that degree of clairvoyance is unnecessary. All that is needed is a reasonably plausible sequence of events and a willingness never to proclaim that such a story represents the only conceivable path to an economic and financial disturbance.

As we observed what was going on in the economy and the financial markets late in 1999, we came up with "The Story So Far. . . ." In it, we imagined a financial disturbance unfolding by April 2000 that would call into question the unabashedly optimistic outlook that the majority of investors, commentators, business executives, and government officials confidently held. It was scripted to proceed along the following lines:

In the months prior to April 2000, when financial markets were jolted by a rush of events that touched off severe turbulence, there had been considerable talk in the papers and in financial circles that the risks were mounting of an unsustainable bubble in the U.S. stock market. Sophisticated investors had begun to consider more seriously that they should be more actively diversifying the currency composition of their global financial assets in order to hedge their bets against a possible setback in the U.S. markets.

Against that background, the immediate trigger of the fictional financial meltdown was described in the written scenario as follows:

> Among the triggering factors were news of a rise in U.S. inflation, prompting market concern of a tightening of American monetary policy, and reports of a sell-off of mutual funds as individuals sought to raise cash to pay higher-than-expected income taxes. Also frequently mentioned by commentators were the announcements by leading personal computer (PC) manufacturers and software providers of a large, unexpected plunge in new orders for their products. Feared problems associated with the Y2K conversion had not materialized. In reassessing their technology needs, business managers from the largest to the smallest enterprises concluded that they had built up sufficient capacity for their operations and could lower new acquisitions by an average of 30 percent. They intended to maintain support for business applications utilizing the Internet. But market optimism about future rapid growth in e-commerce was shaken by a spate of technical glitches that effectively blocked most transactions over the Internet during a sixteen-hour period in late March.

But the simulation needed something more. To transform an ordinary (and not infrequent) downdraft in the financial markets into a rare, full-blown crisis of a magnitude that could endanger the entire system requires something else. What is it?

## From Shock to Crisis: The Role of Accelerants

That was one of the key questions we posed to a distinguished group of financial and policy experts with considerable hands-on experience dealing with past financial crises at a discussion we convened at the Council in September 1999. All participants agreed that a sharp contraction of liquidity was a necessary element in transforming a financial mishap into a full-blown crisis. But in addition there needed to be an *accelerant,* something to spark a process in which the financial markets would be hit by new rounds of pressures that, in turn, would deter private-sector participants from stepping in to provide support. The experts compiled an impressive list of accelerants from past episodes of financial disruption.

One of the most important accelerants they identified was leverage—the direct or indirect use of borrowed funds by investors to enlarge their exposure to market movements. For example, in the 1987 stock market contraction, no one either in the markets or in the regulatory agencies had detailed knowledge of how much leverage there was in the system, what forms it took, who ultimately bore the risks involved, how much risk was hedged, and how reliable those hedges would prove to be. At that time, markets in financial derivatives were developing rapidly, but there was little appreciation of how markets for financial derivatives would behave at a time of stress. Several roundtable participants concurred that this paucity of information became worse as the financial markets grew in complexity. One participant commented: "There is more leverage and less information about it than ever."

A second accelerant might be called forced selling, or involuntary liquidation of equity, bond, currency, or commodity positions. Forced selling has been a recurring theme in many past financial crises. In 1929, forced selling was prevalent in the retail markets because of margin calls. Many investors had been buying stocks on margin; that is, they were borrowing money to buy stocks rather than using their own funds. That leverage magnified profits when the market was rallying but also magnified losses when stock prices fell. Remedial action taken by the U.S. government and the stock exchanges took the form of margin requirements. In principle, the higher the margin requirement, the less leverage, and the less vulnerable an individual investor would be to a sudden fall in stock prices. The authority to set margin requirements was delegated to the Federal Reserve and the Fed retains that responsibility today, although in practice margin requirements are rarely changed.[1]

In 1987, forced selling took the form of what was then known as "portfolio insurance." Investors were promised a buffer against large losses in their equity holdings, and the securities firms that offered the facilities expected to be able to defend themselves through a technique known as dynamic hedging. This was a superficially watertight (but ultimately failed) method of protecting against stock market losses through selling of shares at successively lower prices. In practice, the trades necessary to achieve that happy outcome could not be executed in time and in sufficient size to serve the desired hedging function.[2] In 1998, at the time of the Russian debt default and the subsequent near-collapse of the large hedge fund Long Term Capital Management, forced selling was evident in the unwinding of purportedly hedged positions. In this case, exposures turned out after the fact to be additive rather than offsetting.

To experienced market professionals, the category of forced selling can also encompass a number of familiar trading behaviors that are normally harmless, but can become a source of instability when market conditions become disorderly and liquidity shrinks. For instance, it can reflect the operation of various kinds of trend-following or momentum-based trading systems, in which computers are programmed to issue sell signals to investment managers when the market falls. Forced selling can result from the application of so-called value at risk and similar kinds of statistical models, which large banks and other prominent financial institutions use to control their trading risks. Mutual funds can be subject to a kind of forced selling in response to withdrawals by their investors. Bond managers can be forced to sell fixed-income securities when the credit rating of an issuer is downgraded to below what clients have authorized.

So in addition to positing a reasonably plausible (though certainly not exclusive) triggering mechanism for a market decline, in drafting the scenario to animate our simulation, we also introduced a number of potential accelerants. They took several forms. We injected uncertainties about potential litigation that might impel certain private pension funds to sell stock into an already declining equity market. As described in "The Story So Far . . . ":

> The *Wall Street Journal* published a report asserting that some attorneys had approached regulators in Washington to forewarn them that class action suits were being prepared against a number of the largest private pension funds in the United States for breaching fiduciary duties. The suits would allege that the corporate executives responsible for directing the investment of the pension fund assets had disregarded investment guidelines set by their respective boards of directors. Instead, they had allowed the proportion of equities in their funds' portfolios to rise well above the prescribed limits, essentially by failing to rebalance equity to asset ratios over the period when the stock market was rallying. The news prompted numerous pension fund overseers to take immediate steps to get within their own board guidelines, accentuating the sell-off in the marketplace.

A second accelerant was a by-product of difficulties encountered by a U.S.-based securities affiliate of a major British insurance company. Such an affiliation is not uncommon in the new financial world, in which old demarcations between financial institutions have fallen by the wayside. The scenario revealed that this diversified financial institution had been actively making a market in equity derivatives for hedge funds and other high-octane portfolio managers. This meant that the firm stood ready to buy or sell complex securities or write put or call options on equities or other financial instruments for its clients. When it announced it was temporarily withdrawing from that business pending a thorough review of its exposures, the disclosure had an electrifying effect on an already nervous market. Leveraged equity investors and participants in equity derivatives scrambled to replace maturing contracts that could not be rolled over with either the American affiliate or the British parent.

We purposely did not inject a massive failure of a financial institution, along the lines of the near-collapse of Long Term Capital Management. That policy problem would have been too easy because more than one of the participants in the January simulation had had direct experience with that incident and thus would have been more than well prepared to handle a replica. Because the impact of the more modest program described in the scenario was far more ambiguous, the groups had to evaluate the severity of the problem and decide how much time and effort they should devote to dealing with this problem.

The third accelerant was an inflation scare. The scenario told of a lift in the rate of consumer price inflation in the United States to above 4 percent per year. It also told of "reports that Organization of Petroleum Exporting Countries (OPEC) ministers, meeting in Vienna, had agreed on production cutbacks sufficient to maintain oil prices above the $30 a barrel level."* This was assumed to provoke a sharp increase in yields on long-term government bonds in the United States, Germany, Japan, and other major countries. Crude oil above $30 a barrel seemed to represent both a substantial and a plausible spike in oil prices in December 1999, when the market price was in the low $20s. In hindsight, it turned out to be fairly tame hypothetical level, since the price surged to close to $35 a barrel by March and oscillated around that level for some months thereafter. Interestingly, during 2000, the real-life oil price hike had only a moderately adverse effect on the inflation data and hardly any effect at all on inflationary expectations or the willingness of investors to hold long-term U.S. government bonds. But it did lead briefly to social disruptions in Europe, at one point reminiscent of the 1960s, and abruptly undermined the reputation and political support of more than one European government.

---

* In the simulation we used the West Texas Intermediate Benchmark as a reference, the benchmark for the most frequently traded futures contracts for U.S. energy traders.

Introducing into the scenario more worrying prospects for inflation was done on purpose. We wanted to inject a factor that would tend to make the Federal Reserve's job of crafting an appropriate monetary policy a little harder. After all, participants in the September 1999 roundtable on lessons from past financial crises unanimously cited the need for expanded liquidity as the most important ingredient in stabilizing the markets. We took for granted that such policy action would be taken and said so in "The Story So Far . . . ":

> With uncertainties multiplying, the Federal Reserve issued a statement that it stood ready to inject whatever liquidity was required to protect the safety and soundness of the system.

The Scenario was predicated, however, on the assumption that an injection of liquidity by itself would not be enough to stabilize the markets, and the Fed would be inhibited from easing monetary policy more aggressively because of the upturn in inflation. We also inserted the notion that not everybody agreed with the Fed's course. According to "The Story So Far . . . ":

> The European Central Bank ended its scheduled policy meeting without a public expression of support for the Fed's action. Two members of the ECB privately told journalists that they were concerned about the potential moral hazard engendered by an "asymmetric" policy toward asset prices, as seemed to be practiced by the U.S. central bank.

A fourth accelerant came through the foreign exchange markets. Here is what the simulation participants were told.

> Concerned that the Federal Reserve was abandoning an anti-inflationary stance and confused about ECB intentions, foreign exchange dealers rushed to sell dollars and buy euros, even as they continued to build up even larger plus positions in Japanese yen. The dollar consequently fell sharply in the foreign exchange markets, while Bloomberg News carried reports of a spike in

U.S. import prices, after five years in which import prices had continuously declined.

Against this background, the economic, financial, and monetary policy experts had their work cut out for them. The central bankers had to weigh the dangers of worsening the nascent inflationary pressures by lowering short-term interest rates too much, creating excess liquidity, and hurting the dollar against the dangers of failing to come to grips with a deteriorating situation in stock and bond markets. The financial regulators had to consider the merits and demerits of closing the markets, or setting up new or toughened circuit breakers, while finding out whether various institutions were in danger of failing and making a bad situation even worse. The economic and trade policy group had to worry about whether to intervene to support the value of the dollar in the foreign exchange markets and to head off possible protectionist pressures. Above all, the cabinet-level officers and congressional leaders had to craft a political strategy for dealing with a potentially severe erosion in public confidence that could help spawn a contraction in consumer spending and business investment.

## The Market Setting

Among the numerous financial measures that market participants follow on a minute-to-minute basis, we selected eight to give a snapshot of the state of the markets: the familiar Dow Jones industrial average; the high-tech-heavy Nasdaq composite index; two indicators of foreign stock market behavior, Japan's Nikkei stock index and Germany's DAX index; the yield on thirty-year U.S. Treasury bonds, a closely watched and heavily traded instrument that has long served as a shorthand proxy for the fixed-income market in the United States; the price of crude oil, as depicted by the price of the West Texas Intermediate (WTI) Crude benchmark; and two measures of developments in the foreign exchange markets, the dollar vs. the yen and the euro

| Financial indicator | Actual market values on January 21, 2000 (day before the simulation) | Hypothetical values for fictional scenario *July 3, 2000* |
|---|---|---|
| Dow Jones industrial average | 11,251 | 8,800 |
| Nasdaq | 4,235 | 3,235 |
| Nikkei, Japan | 18,878 | 16,800 |
| DAX, Germany | 6,992 | 5,000 |
| Thirty-year U.S. treasury bond *Yield to maturity* | 6.81% | 7.50% |
| WTI crude oil *U.S. $ per barrel* | $29.80 | $31 |
| Japanese yen per U.S. dollar | ¥105.2 | ¥92 |
| U.S. dollar per euro | $0.9980 | $1.07 |

vs. the dollar. The table above shows where these variables stood in the marketplace on January 21, 2000, the day before the simulation was held on January 22, 2000, and where the fictional scenario put them as of the future date (July 3, 2000) when the clock on the scoreboard of the game was scripted to begin.

See Appendix E for a graphical display of the movements in these financial instruments over the twelve-month period from January 21, 1999, to January 21, 2000, the hypothesized fluctuations during the intervening January 22–July 3 time period, and the fictional daily and weekly movements over the course of the game.

## At the Simulation—Part I

Within the American government, the main day-to-day responsibility for influencing short-term fluctuations in the economy rests with the central bank, the Federal Reserve System. Our Central Banking Group included current and former Fed talent and went about its work with professionalism and a firm grasp of institutional traditions. It is very important to understand the point of view of the Fed when financial markets are troubled, as Central Banking Group chair John Heimann explained at the mid-day simulated press conference (undoubtedly echoing the real-life Fed chair, Alan Greenspan):

> Number one, first and foremost, is to do no harm. Any action that is not thoughtful, that is not kept in line with the broad perspective of achieving economic growth in this country and the world, would not be helpful. Secondly, our view is long-term, stable economic growth, with an eye to keeping inflation under control.

The key to good decision-making within the Federal Reserve is to amass a tremendous amount of detailed data on the status of the U.S. economy and the financial markets and then attempt to gauge, as accurately as it can, how financial markets will respond both to Fed actions and to Fed words. Another crucial element is conducting ongoing discussions with counterparts at central banks in other countries, traditionally the Bank of England, the Deutsche Bundesbank, the Banque de France, and the Bank of Japan. Nowadays, interchange of information and views with the brand new European central bank is especially important. The Central Bankers in the simulation, true to life, were tireless in their efforts to pry detailed information on the economy and the financial markets out of the Control Room. They were equally relentless in their quest to interact with foreign central banks. They put a characteristic emphasis not only on reaching decisions on setting interest rates and providing liquidity but also on how best to craft the written communiqués that unveiled this information to the public (and the rest of the government). A stated goal of the Control Room Group was to provide information about their actions, without contributing to any unease or panic in the markets.

At the beginning of the exercise, the central bankers were confronted with a dilemma. Financial markets were shaky. Stock prices had fallen sharply, but from what had been widely viewed by a number of experts (if not the majority) as unsustainably high levels. Moreover, the latest information suggested that the plunge in the stock market might be over. In the credit markets, long-term interest rates, which the Fed does not directly control, were on the rise. Traders cited the worsening of inflationary expectations, as oil prices rose and the value of the U.S. dollar against other countries started to slip. Yet, the overall U.S. economy, while decelerating, was still operating at a high level. The fictional figures given out indicated growth in real GDP of 3.5 percent per annum in the first quarter and 1 percent in the second quarter. The unemployment rate had drifted up to 4.75 percent. The consumer price index was increasing at 4 percent per annum. And credit problems in the corporate sector had not yet surfaced, as evidenced by relatively modest spreads between yields on U.S. Treasury securities and yields on corporate bonds of below-average credit quality.

The decision of the Central Banking Group was to maintain the target for the Fed's funds rate at the then present rate of 6 percent but also to announce that the American central bank stood ready to inject liquidity into the banking system through standard operating procedures should additional liquidity be needed. In short, the Central Bankers started out giving roughly equal weight to stabilizing the financial markets and to preventing an acceleration of inflation. Moreover, they also advised the other groups that the exchange rates in existence at the time did not require immediate action, and thus foreign exchange intervention was not needed. In the simulation, the Economics and Trade Group combined the functions of the U.S. Treasury and the U.S. Trade Representative. In the real world, Treasury normally has the final say on foreign exchange rates and intervention policy. In the simulation, the members of the Economics and Trade Group did not disagree with the central bankers' assessment.

That posture started to change somewhat as new information flowed in, and the political context came to the fore. In a dramatic departure from intergovernmental norms during past real-world financial crises, Mario Baeza, treasury secretary, took the initiative to visit the central bank's headquarters in order to discuss in person the various worrisome problems that the U.S. authorities were collectively facing, including the possibility that American consumers would become more cautious in their spending behavior as a result of the nose dive in equity prices. The result of this collaboration was an agreement that, together, the Treasury and the Fed would issue a general joint statement aimed at calming the markets. For its part, the Central Banking Group issued the following statement to the public:

> In keeping with the forward-looking character of monetary policy, the Federal Open Market Committee has reduced the target federal funds rate from 6 percent to 5.5 percent—thus reversing the increase that occurred in the first half of the year—in order to forestall any tendency for recent developments to lead to a contraction of economic activity in the United States.*

Over the rest of the first half of the simulation—in other words, over the next week to ten days in game time—as the world financial markets experienced several bouts of renewed turbulence, the central bankers peppered the Control Room with questions on how the financial markets were functioning.

> *Question*: What was the nature of the selling in the stock and bond markets? Was the selling done by individuals or by large institutions such as hedge funds, pension funds, or insurance companies?
>
> *Answer*: There was major selling of retail mutual funds by individuals, while institutions were mixed in their trading patterns.

* The FOMC is the Fed's internal body that is responsible for making monetary policy decisions. It is composed of the members of the Board of Governors in Washington, the president of the Federal Reserve Bank of New York, and four other Reserve Bank presidents who serve on a rotating basis, but all of whom take part in policy discussions.

*Question*: Were there bids in the markets for financial derivatives—forwards, futures, swaps, and options?

*Answer*: Currency and bond futures and options markets were operating normally but there were major question marks about over-the-counter trading in derivatives based on equities.

*Question*: How about the volume of turnover in the various segments of the financial markets?

*Answer*: The market for U.S. Treasuries was thin, with even relatively small trades precipitating substantial movements in bond prices and yields. Trading in U.S. corporate bonds was very weak. There was hardly any trading going on of existing emerging market debt. But exceptionally large volumes were being bought and sold in foreign currency markets.

*Question*: What was happening to economies abroad?

*Answer*: Generally businesses appeared to be cutting back on capital expenditures, and retail sales were starting to slide.

As the simulation proceeded, trading was reported to be tense and unsettled. Thus, the U.S. central bankers reached out to their counterparts in Europe at the European Central Bank. The scenario showed that the ECB had left short-term interest rates unchanged and that there was some criticism of U.S. monetary policy within that institution. "The Story So Far . . ." explained that "the European Central Bank ended its scheduled policy meeting without a public expression of support for the Fed's action. Two members of the ECB privately told journalists that they were concerned about the potential moral hazard engendered by an 'asymmetric' policy toward asset prices, as seemed to be practiced by the U.S. central bank." At least some Europeans were critical of the asymmetry that the Fed had not tried to tighten credit conditions preemptively while the U.S. stock market was booming but appeared to be eager to ease liquidity while the market was setting back.

After the cut in the federal funds rate to 5.5 percent, members of the Central Banking Group asked the ECB (played by the Control Room): "Do you agree that this is the appropriate time for joint action for a modest reduction in interest rates" to deal with the reemergence of disorderly financial market conditions? The answer from the ECB was "No, the euro is still too weak. The ECB would contemplate joint action only in the event that the euro appreciates back above $1.10." According to the fictional data, the euro exchange rate with respect to the dollar was only $1.05 at the time. So there was no immediate agreement for a coordinated interest rate response. It was clear to all that the Europeans were content to let the erosion of confidence in the U.S. financial markets spill over onto the U.S. dollar so that they could enjoy a rebound in the long beleaguered euro.

As for the Japanese, they were said to be preparing a broad policy initiative but were not ready yet to report all the details. "The Story So Far . . . " asserted that the Japanese had told the U.S. financial authorities of their frustration over the lack of stability in the yen-dollar currency market, despite sizable Japanese official intervention. They said Japan was no longer capable of taking the entire exchange rate risk of its dollar support. At a minimum, Japan wanted to get in on any special facilities the United States instituted for other countries. In the meantime, the Japanese authorities were establishing a study group to analyze the potential policy benefits of imposing a tax on large bank deposits.

During the simulation, the Japanese authorities provided some elaboration on their motives. The so-called negative interest penalty, which would only apply to deposits above ten million yen, was fashioned on a similar program conducted by the Swiss authorities during the 1970s. It would be designed to discourage speculation in the yen. The Japanese were also considering ways to impose a tax on transactions in foreign currency derivatives, akin to proposals made in the past by Yale University economics professor and Nobel laureate James Tobin.* Market sources informed the U.S. authorities that, if enacted, the negative interest penalty would appear to have a disproportionately adverse

---

* In 1972, James Tobin proposed imposing a tax of 0.1 to .25 percent on cross-border currency trading. The goal was to cut the destabilizing potential of short-term speculation and restrain big money markets. Proponents believe it could help emerging countries in times of financial difficulty.

impact on foreign institutions that traditionally rely more heavily on wholesale sources of funding than on retail deposits. When the announcement of this part of the study group agenda came across the wires, the initial impact was to spur further demand for yen in the foreign exchange markets. The Decision-Makers Group was sufficiently baffled by the Japanese policy stance to ask the simulation groups whether the United States should encourage or discourage the Japanese authorities from going ahead with either of these initiatives.

All groups opposed the initiatives, but with subtle differences in tone. The Financial Regulatory Group told the Decision-Makers Group they would strongly discourage the Japanese initiatives. They were particularly concerned that such measures were contrary to the principle of national treatment.* They also called attention to the potential negative impact on Japan itself. It might end up harming the funding and liquidity of Japanese banks, which could have further negative implications for liquidity throughout Asia. And if the stock market in Tokyo reacted negatively, it could further weaken the capital base of Japanese banks, since through cross ownership they owned many shares of Japanese corporations.

The Economics and Trade Group disagreed with the Ministry of Finance and Bank of Japan's hypothesis that a "negative interest penalty" would be a productive means of dealing with the appreciation of the yen. The group thought that it might easily backfire. But, they concluded that publicly criticizing the analytical direction of the proposed study group might not be the best way of getting the Japanese authorities to scuttle the idea. Instead, they suggested it would be more constructive to offer to participate in the study group provided it examined a variety of means

---

* National Treatment is defined as "the commitment by a country to treat enterprises operating on its territory, but controlled by the nationals of another country, no less favourably than domestic enterprises in like situations. This commitment is enshrined in the Declaration on International Investment and Multinational Enterprises, adopted in 1976 by the governments of the OECD member countries." *National Treatment for Foreign-Controlled Enterprises: Decision of the Council Including Member Countries' Exceptions to National Treatment* (Paris: Organisation for Economic Cooperation and Development, 1995), 2.

to address the problem of the rising yen, beyond just the negative interest penalty.

As the first part of the simulation drew to a close, the Central Banking Group issued an official statement:

> The Federal Reserve System is closely monitoring both financial and fundamental economic developments. The system is continuously in contact with the relevant foreign authorities, as well as with the financial markets. The System is also well aware of the concerns raised by recent increases in market volatility. The stance of monetary policy, in the wake of the recent ½ percent reduction in short-term interest rates, is fully consistent with promoting economic growth in the United States, fostering stability in U.S. financial markets, and supporting efforts abroad to stabilize foreign markets and economies.

Soon after, the top cabinet officials, White House staff, and congressional leadership that made up the Decision-Makers Group gave a background briefing to the press to explain their own efforts to bring about an end to the crisis. Jim Jones, who chaired the Decision-Makers Group and played the role of national security adviser, told the reporters that the task the decision-makers set for themselves was "what do we do about the general level of confidence that has been dropping very precipitously in the country." He went on to elaborate their thinking and the plans they were making to revive confidence in the markets and in the nation:

> As the financial crisis developed, the president initially remained silent to avoid making things worse. But as the situation has dragged on and spread out throughout the world, he has decided that it is now time to give a speech designed to do several things. Number one, to clearly establish that this problem is not a Democratic or a Republican problem. This is an American problem, and it is a global problem. The United States cannot escape its leadership responsibilities, and to exercise them we must really be united and not divided. Number two, while there is no intention to

ignore the swings in the stock market, the president will follow
up on the Federal Reserve's statement to assure the public that
the fundamentals of this economy are truly sound. Number three,
he will outline a number of steps to restore confidence. For example, the president has contacted many of the world leaders to tell
them about the measures that we will be taking, to get feedback
from them, and to solicit their support. We seek their cooperation
and their sense of unity that we're in this together.

Furthermore, he will be calling in the congressional leadership
and working with them toward preserving a unified American
position. Soon, he will also convene a "wise persons group" made
up of experienced, respected Americans—the Bob Rubins, the
Colin Powells, the George Schultzs, and many others—to work
together on a bipartisan basis to accomplish a couple of important
and difficult tasks. First is to dispatch these individuals to areas
of the world where they are particularly well equipped to deal
with the foreign leadership. They will be able to convey a sense
of confidence that we in the U.S. government know what we're
doing, that we're moving forward with a strong plan, and that
we want their support and their help in building support around
the world. Second is to work with our Congress on a regular
basis to review where we are and what we're doing, as well
as to answer the plethora of questions that may come up from
individual members of Congress and their constituents on a
daily basis.

These themes echoed the conclusions of the members of the
Economics and Trade Group, chaired by Richard Goeltz. The
group stressed the need for political leaders to decide that stabilizing the financial markets and preventing a further erosion of
confidence was an objective that must have bipartisan support,
not partisan bickering. However, the group was skeptical about
the value of overt intervention in the financial markets. As Goeltz
told simulation participants in their plenary session: "The global
capital markets and communications technology that link those
markets are changing so rapidly that the sums for stabilization
that were effective in the past could easily be swamped by events

today. It is in our long-term best interest to begin to assemble adequate resources at the government level and at the supranational level *now* so we can be better prepared to deal with future crises."

John Whitehead, who played the role of secretary of state, laid out the foreign policy actions that needed to be taken during the period when domestic policies to stabilize the financial situation were developed and implemented. His reasoning was as follows:

There were a number of other foreign policy questions that did come up and that had to be answered each in its own way. We were very conscious that we were not only heading our own department, but we were in effect representing the president, as the president's principal advisers in these various areas of defense and finance and foreign policy. So, we tried to make sure that all of this information kept flowing to us from all of you who are advising us constantly on what was happening and what new action you advised us to take.

We tried to be sure that the president didn't get diverted from what we thought was the major problem that the country faced at this particular time, which was the potential economic collapse of the United States and, very likely, of the whole world. With stock markets down by one-third from their high points at the beginning of the year, the American people had suffered huge losses, had experienced a tremendous loss of confidence and were indeed alarmed about their situation. Though the official statistics will only come out with a lag, we assumed that, with a drop in the stock market like that, people were not buying their third car, or their second home, as quickly as they had before. We may even be on the verge of a serious recession or depression—maybe more than on the verge.

So, we advised the president to focus on that particular issue and not allow these other relatively small issues to interfere with his expression of his primary concern. When we were talking about his speech that is now under way, it featured the economic situation and had him focus on that, rather than on the miscellaneous issues that were occurring around the world at the same time that this economic collapse was beginning.

Finally, beyond fighting the brush fires that flared up, I think that the main task for foreign policymakers can be defined in simple terms. It was trying to be sure that every nation affected by anything that we did was notified and hopefully persuaded that what we were going to do was in their interest, as well as in ours, or at least that they understood why we were doing it. That was the main concern that, as secretary of state, I tried to allay.

The first half of the simulation presented a set of circumstances that could have led to a more narrowly nationalistic policy response, along the lines of seeking to attend to the financial pressures in U.S. markets, while letting the rest of the world fend for itself. That course was not followed. Instead, the participants appeared to accept the global feedback as both conditioning and constraining U.S. policy options. Thus, they were prepared to follow a broad internationally minded approach, even when other countries were slow to go along with U.S. leadership or to challenge it.

## At the Simulation—Part II:
## More Work to Stabilize the System

Despite the best efforts of the government and central banks of the United States and the other major industrial countries, financial markets stayed in turmoil. The table on the next page shows how key financial variables moved during the first part of the simulation.

As participants headed into the second half of the simulation, stock markets were still unsteady, long-term bond yields fluctuated erratically, the dollar remained under pressure against other major currencies in the foreign exchange markets, and the price of oil was tending to rise further. The specter of another sharp fall in the value of the financial wealth of Americans had not been completely eliminated.

Moreover, the terrible economic consequences of the loss of wealth that had already occurred were now apparent. Simulation

| Financial indicator | Hypothetical values at the start of Part I *July 3, 2000* | Hypothetical values at the end of Part I *July 14, 2000* |
|---|---|---|
| Dow Jones industrial average | 8,800 | 7,700 |
| Nasdaq | 3,235 | 2,800 |
| Nikkei, Japan | 16,800 | 17,000 |
| DAX, Germany | 5,000 | 5,200 |
| Thirty-year U.S. treasury bond *Yield to maturity* | 7.50% | 7.70% |
| WTI crude oil *U.S. $ per barrel* | $31 | $33 |
| Japanese yen per U.S. dollar | ¥92 | ¥90 |
| U.S. dollar per euro | $1.07 | $1.12 |

participants learned that the estimate for third-quarter real GDP was a sharp 3 percent decline in output, the worst outcome since the deep recession of the early 1980s. Unemployment was rising quickly, consumer confidence was evaporating, and businesses were reviewing investment plans with an eye toward cutting back all but high priority projects. Financial institutions reported a 20 percent surge in delinquencies on credit card debt and mortgages. A large foreign financial conglomerate was said to be close to failure, with possible repercussions on its U.S. affiliate.

Political effects were also evident. Newly released public opinion polls showed a 20 percentage point drop in the president's approval rating. (That was thought to be rather extreme at the time, but it was a little less than that actually suffered by Prime Minister Tony Blair in the week after the disruption of gasoline supplies in Britain!) The November 2000 presidential election would be a dead heat. The same polls indicated that support for the Republican Party in the congressional election had soared to the point where Republicans would gain a veto-proof majority in the Senate.

The White House staff had been asked by the president to convene an immediate meeting of his economic and foreign policy advisers to develop a "bold new plan for reviving confidence and reasserting U.S. leadership in the world."

## Monetary Policy Shifts Gears

The receipt of new economic data had a powerful impact on deliberations of the FOMC. The central bankers decided that the risks in the economy had shifted dramatically and that a substantial reduction in short-term rates was essential to righting the incipient downturn. In the debate, one member demanded to know "What should we do when banks begin to fail?" Noting the lessons that could be drawn from our experiences of the 1930s, a debate began over the importance of sustaining "sick" banks. One participant argued that the discount window was no longer an effective tool; however, others disagreed and noted that one possible policy response to failing banks would be to change the collateralization requirements for borrowing at the discount window. The group also discussed the possibility of approaching decision-makers within the Financial Regulatory Group to discuss regulatory forbearance in the closing down of troubled banks—to avoid a repeat of the 1930s. The question then was asked, "What would we do if the FDIC was lacking in sufficient funds to save failing banks?"

These concerns over a possible ugly repeat of history may have helped to trigger the Central Banking Group's decision to move rates by 150 basis points (i.e., 1.5 percentage points). Such a forceful action was not unchallenged within the group. One participant noted that a move of just 1 percent would be viewed by the market as "aggressive." Another noted that a move of 1.5 percent might "scare people." However, the group was swayed in favor of taking such a large step by the member who observed that "people were already scared."

Accordingly, the federal funds rate was lowered from 5.5 percent to 4 percent. Later on, as the economic reports available to the Central Banking Group continued to sour, the group followed up with another 100 basis point cut to 3 percent—the level that last prevailed early in the 1990s in the aftermath of the savings and loan crisis and the collapse of the commercial real estate market in much of the country.

The American central bankers also sought to work on the international dimension of restoring financial stability. A meeting with the central bank governors of the other major industrial countries was requested to review the situation and question whether they had any plans for common action. The Central Banking Group also noted that there were a number of unresolved issues regarding financial difficulties in Brazil, real estate financing problems in Germany, and a threat of bank failures in Turkey that would also be worthwhile discussing.

Central bank officials in Europe quickly responded, by way of the Control Room. They reminded the Americans that the European Central Bank had lowered interest rates—as promised—when the euro had climbed above $1.10, and they were contemplating further modest reductions in interest rates. But they noted that "our household sector is not invested much in stocks and thus does not get directly hurt." Thus, they discounted the so-called wealth effect as a pressing problem for Europe.* However, they agreed that the Brazilian, German, and Turkish cases deserved close scrutiny. While there seemed to be progress toward solutions in the first two cases, the Turkish banking problem was "very dangerous" and was being followed "very carefully" both by the ECB and by European Union (EU) governments.

---

* The wealth effect is popularly defined as "an increase in consumer spending based on the perceived wealth created by the escalating value of stock market portfolios." From the online dictionary "Wordspy" http://www.logophilia.com/WordSpy/wealtheffect.html.

## The Fiscal Policy Option

Meanwhile, the Control Room reported that the president was getting more and more impatient. Monetary policy steps were welcome. They were timely and forceful. But they were not in themselves sufficient to revive consumer confidence; politically that mattered a great deal. So the president took the initiative to instruct his advisers to consider broadening the stabilization strategy to include a major fiscal policy initiative.

After years, even decades, of large and unpopular budget deficits, which essentially inactivated any fiscal policy option, there initially was little enthusiasm to take up that task. However, market developments began to push simulation participants in the direction of fiscal stimulus. That was because the Federal Reserve's bold reduction of interest rates was precipitating an across-the-board fall in the value of the dollar. And expectations of further dollar declines were generating sizable outflows of foreign investments from U.S. capital markets, which were weighing on stock and bond prices. Fiscal stimulus, by taking some of the burden for stabilizing the economy off the Fed, could help to strengthen the dollar—or at least cushion its slide.

Thus, the Decision-Makers Group requested a formal recommendation from the Economics and Trade Group on how to advise the president. For a time, the members of the latter group were divided on what to recommend. All agreed on the wisdom of lowering interest rates, as the Fed was doing. There was agreement on increasing some areas of federal spending. But viewpoints diverged materially on the core issue of how to use fiscal policy to stimulate the economy and reassure the financial markets, reflecting differences in political and economic philosophies not easily reconciled. One part of the group believed that the government should take this opportunity to protect those who would be hit hardest by the financial and now economic crisis, recommending expanded health care coverage and lower taxes for the poor. Others believed that stimulating domestic industry and encouraging foreign investment in the United States with tax breaks would be more instrumental in reversing the crisis. At least one participant insisted that any tax cutting should be explicitly temporary, with a clear sunset provision, on the argument that before the financial crisis hit, the economy was operating close to full capacity and that when markets settled down and confidence returned, strong economic growth would likely resume. Permanent tax cuts would then threaten to re-ignite inflationary pressures and compel a potentially destabilizing tightening of monetary policy.

After vigorous discussion, the Economics and Trade Group agreed on a policy position that included the following elements:

> The president should recommend to the Congress a temporary fiscal stimulus package of about $135 billion, roughly 1.5 percent of GDP. The package would be expected to do the following:

- Exempt from income tax anyone with a personal income of less than $20,000 per year.
- Lower marginal tax rates for the two lowest income tax brackets by 1 percent per year.
- Front-load this year's government expenditures to increase domestic employment.
- Convene a meeting with state governors to encourage them to consider temporary reductions in state sales taxes.
- Extend compensation periods for unemployment benefits.
- Extend low-cost health insurance to the unemployed and to low-income individuals.
- Lower the tax on dividend income to 50 percent of its current level to raise the after-tax rate of return on equities.
- Eliminate withholding taxes on foreign investments in U.S. securities.

> The president should also meet with foreign heads of state to ensure the free flow of goods, services, and investments around the world.

As the simulation neared its end, the Decision-Makers Group authorized a press release based on this recommendation that laid out key elements of a new fiscal program:

> The administration has determined to erect a test program for lowering marginal income tax rates for low- and middle-income people and reducing the earned income tax credit threshold. It will be expanding federal government spending in a number of areas, including establishment of a new program to extend health care benefits to the unemployed. Moreover, state governors are being invited to the White House to discuss a temporary sales tax rebate. Finally, expressing confidence that the fundamentals of the U.S. economy are sound and the United States is well-positioned to respond to the present economic and financial crisis, the president is proposing a 50 percent cut in taxation of dividend income and the elimination of any withholding taxes on foreign investments in U.S. financial assets.

Leaks that the president would be announcing a fiscal program spawned dramatic headlines on all the major wire services: "Ambitious Fiscal Policy Initiative in the Works." Markets rallied strongly on the news. Later, the following background alert was distributed to members of the media:

> The president is about to make a speech outlining his fiscal stimulus program. He will declare that the economy is sound and the measures he is proposing will help restore it to its customary excellent growth performance. The programs are designed to help those who have suffered from the recent slowdown. There will be an ongoing dialogue among the executive branch, members of Congress, governors, and business and labor leaders.

The table on the next page shows that by the end of the simulation most markets had recovered—but only to the approximate levels prevailing at the beginning of the game. The sell-off between April and July 2000 had yet to be reversed.

| Financial indicator | Hypothetical values at the start of Part II *July 15, 2000* | Hypothetical values at the end of Part II *Oct. 6, 2000* |
|---|---|---|
| Dow Jones industrial average | 7,600 | 8,800 |
| Nasdaq | 2,900 | 3,235 |
| Nikkei, Japan | 18,000 | 19,000 |
| DAX, Germany | 5,000 | 5,500 |
| Thirty-year U.S. treasury bond *Yield to maturity* | 6.9% | 7.5% |
| WTI crude oil *U.S. $ per barrel* | $35 | $38 |
| Japanese yen per U.S. dollar | ¥82 | ¥85 |
| U.S. dollar per euro | $1.20 | $1.15 |

## Notes

1.  Louis Loss, *Securities Regulation* (New York: Little Brown & Co. Law and Business, 1991).

2.  U.S. Presidential Task Force on Market Mechanisms (Washington, D.C.: U.S. Government Printing Office, 1988); commonly known as the Brady Commission Report.

# Chapter III

# Mexico in Flux: Trouble in the Neighborhood

## Real-World Backdrop

Coming into the new century, the Mexican economic, financial, and political situation was in flux. There were some unmistakable positive developments. Lifted by the strong economic growth in the United States, Mexican export-oriented industries were booming. The rebound in oil prices was helping to generate higher government revenues, so long-standing budgetary problems appeared more manageable. The credit quality of Mexican debt was seen to be improving, and one of the major ratings agencies had upgraded the credit rating of outstanding Mexican government bonds. This had a favorable effect on Mexican financial markets. In fact, during 1999, the combination of a firmer Mexican peso exchange rate and a spurt of Mexican equity prices had generated impressive returns of well over 50 percent to U.S. dollar-based investors.

Despite these improvements, plenty of vulnerabilities remained. The remnants of past financial disasters had not been sorted out, and the domestic banking system remained weak, undercapitalized, and unable to play a dynamic role in financing new business ventures. Struggling domestically oriented businesses, most without access to fresh credit, were unable to survive without large-scale official support. Yet, the vehicle that had been established to work out the problem of troubled loans, the Banking Fund for the Protection of Savings, known by the Spanish acronym FOBAPROA, had turned out to be dysfunctional and corrupt, a political albatross.* So the Mexican government essentially had to start over by establishing in May 1999 a new mechanism for bailing out the banks and their heavily indebted customers, called the IPAB.** Social stability faced severe challenges as well, and not only in the remote state of Chiapas, where a low-grade rebellion led by the shadowy, but romantic, figure known as Sub-commandante Marcos had dragged on since the mid-1990s. To many Mexicans, the sense of spinning out of control was even more graphically symbolized by the nearly yearlong, and occasionally violent, strike by radical elements at Universidad Nacional Autónoma de México, UNAM, the huge public university in Mexico City. To others, it was most clearly evidenced by the frequent kidnappings and seemingly unstoppable drug-related violence.

By January 2000, Mexico was already immersed in its own presidential election campaign. The Partido Revolucionario Institucional, the PRI, had run Mexican politics for nearly three-quarters of the twentieth century but under the leadership of President Ernesto Zedillo and his intrepid band of reformers, things were beginning to open up. The PRI candidate, Francisco Labastida, was selected in a national primary election, and he came out of that experiment in modern democracy with a convincing lead in the public opinion polls over Vicente Fox, the ambitious and charismatic candidate of the center-right PAN party. But many Mexican political observers felt that Fox had

* FOBAPROA stands for "Fondo Bancario de Protección al Ahorro."
** IPAB stands for "Instituto para la Protección al Ahorro Bancario."

personal qualities and policy positions that could close the gap and present Mexican voters with a genuine choice.

## The Story So Far . . .

"The Story So Far . . ." was constructed so that the game would start in early July, right after the Mexican election. In reading the scenario, simulation participants learned of a string of complex and potentially dangerous fictional events that had occurred in the interim:

> Mexico was in the middle of a hotly contested presidential election when market volatility suddenly escalated. The confidence that Mexico was starting to overcome long-standing banking and economic problems quickly evaporated, and the hesitant response of the Mexican government, as well as the PRI presidential candidate, did little to reassure domestic and foreign investors. Support for the PAN's candidate picked up, as middle class Mexicans told pollsters that there was a pressing need for new leadership to guide the country through troubled economic times. The outcome of the election was a virtual dead heat, with scattered violence at polling places and charges of voting irregularities by all three political parties. Rumors swirled of a surge of illegal immigrants seeking to enter the United States. Correspondents of U.S. and European news organizations who tried to cover this breaking story were said to have been detained by the Mexican authorities. The Washington bureaus of the *New York Times* and CNN revealed that senior members of the House of Representatives, including both Democrats and Republicans, had warned the administration not to recognize a winner prematurely. Some powerful Republican committee chairmen in the U.S. Senate were even said to be pressing the State Department to identify the PAN candidate as the victor.

Thus, the scenario hypothesized a direct link between the financial meltdown (which had originated in the United States but was spreading globally) and a rupture in political-social stability across the border. Opponents of the North American

Free Trade Agreement (NAFTA) had long been prepared to exploit the American public's anxiety over the immigration issue and over Mexico's commitment to democratization, more generally.

Moreover, other complications were added to the spectacle, some of which echoed actual events that had taken place in Mexico during the long-standing UNAM strike. As reported in "The Story So Far . . .":

> The political drama unfolding in the Mexican election inflamed already existing passions on the nation's campuses. The more than year-old stalemate at UNAM flared up again, spreading more forcefully than before to other Mexican educational institutions and spawning sporadic disorder. There were incidents of blockaded highways, some arson, and scattered gunfire.

Against this background, the scenario envisioned a novel form of linkage—that is, between cyber-terrorism and the safety and soundness of the financial system. Here is how it was described in "The Story So Far . . .":

> A small group of computer hackers siding with the well-armed radicals, and financed by an organization thought to have ties to associates of Venezuelan President Hugo Chávez, had managed to tap into the computers of the second largest Mexican bank, possibly with the help of disgruntled employees. It was the same bank that some months before the onset of global financial turbulence had completed negotiations for a historic merger with one of the five leading U.S. banking organizations. This had been shrilly opposed by a variety of Mexicans, including those opposed to globalization in general and those who resist tighter links between Mexican and American companies. The hackers published a website displaying a variety of embarrassing data, including detailed information on non-performing loans that far exceeded the amounts that the Mexican bank had previously disclosed, as well as the numbers of secret accounts controlled by leading political and judicial figures. Mexican financial markets

were roiled by reports that the U.S. bank was threatening to withdraw from the merger in view of the leaked information.

## At the Simulation

Right after the simulation began, simulation participants were asked to develop U.S. policy responses to each of the plot lines. The assignments went along functional lines. For example, the Financial Regulatory Group and the Central Banking Group were asked to respond to questions about the bank merger that was about to fall through, while the Foreign Policy and National Security Group was asked what U.S. policy should be toward the hung election and the surge of illegal immigration it may have triggered.

## Tackling the Policy Problems

The uniform reaction of all the groups was to calm troubled waters. Both the Decision-Makers Group and the Foreign Policy and National Security Group took a detached perspective on the hung election, despite confirmation of extensive electoral fraud. They felt it was for the Mexicans to sort out themselves. The U.S. government would not weigh in by expressing a preference. The State Department would issue a statement looking forward to a good working relationship with the new Mexican president. Similarly, the decision-makers were not inclined to get involved with any aspect of Mexico's banking problems and were content to allow the expert groups to proceed as they thought best. The U.S. central bankers issued a statement indicating that they had talked to the management of the U.S. bank and encouraged them to postpone any merger plans until the question of the veracity of the accounting irregularities was cleared up. They noted that the problem was limited to those particular institutions and was not a systemic issue for either the U.S. or the Mexican financial systems.

From the political perspective, however, the reports of a surge of illegal immigrants to the U.S. border was a source of alarm for the Decision-Makers Group. After intense discussion, they decided to recommend that the president should contact incumbent President Zedillo, alert him to the political delicacy of the border-control issue, and commit the United States to beefing up border patrols. But adequate policing of the border might require National Guard or U.S. military units since order on the Mexican side was bound to be dubious.

## The Control Room Perspective

Several senior advisers leaving the U.S. government over the past few years have commented that U.S.-Mexican policy is increasingly being domesticized. That means when issues arise, fewer go through traditional State Department diplomatic channels and more and more go through domestic agencies, such as Agriculture, Transportation, the Environmental Protection Agency, the Drug Enforcement Administration, or the Federal Bureau of Investigation. That shift was evident in the simulation as well. Plot elements involving Mexico were in effect delegated to a particular agency based on technical competence rather than broader foreign policy–security considerations. But there was one exception: the issue of a migration surge. That was clearly viewed as a national security threat and a test of our foreign relations. Thus, the Decision-Makers Group dealt quickly and forcefully to contain its potential adverse consequences.

In the real world, cultural and political events in Mexico went very differently than the scenario portrayal. In the July 2000 Mexican election, conventional wisdom of late 1999 and early 2000—that the PRI would easily hold the presidency—was turned upside down. Vicente Fox prevailed by a convincing margin in an election that was devoid of incident or irregularities, just as President Zedillo and his team had foreseen. The transition to a Fox presidency was harmonious rather than combative, although by the spring of 2001 sharp policy disagreements between President Fox and the opposition majority in the Mexican Congress were occurring with some frequency.

As for the fictional rumors in the simulation of Venezuelan President Chávez meddling in Mexican affairs, they have not materialized. To the contrary, President Fox has opened a dialogue with the Venezuelan leader. But in fact occasional rumors have surfaced in the financial markets from time to time that President Chávez or his admirers have been involved in political events in other South American countries. The most frequently heard related to events in Ecuador in January 2000, when the presidential palace was assaulted, the president resigned under pressure, and a new president, Gustavo Noboa, was installed.

Finally, events that appear to be technical matters that should be delegated to experts in the regulatory agencies take on broader significance. One example is the "hackers" story. It provides a glimpse of how priorities can change when hypothetical events actually happen. At the time the scenario was drafted late in 1999, a major cyber attack against e-commerce seemed more like science fiction than a pressing concern. No longer. Since the simulation took place in January 2000, there have been serious incidents of cyber-vandalism, one of which virtually closed down some of the largest websites in the world (the notorious "love bug" virus). We all appreciate that similar threats—or worse— will be a permanent feature of the business landscape and one that will challenge future security experts and policymakers, both in the private sector and in government.

# Chapter IV

# Saudi Arabia Coming-of-Age: When Allies Start Going Their Own Way

## Real-World Backdrop

Saudi Arabia presents an enigma. The largest oil producer and home to most of the world's oil reserves, its strategic importance is unsurpassed. The Gulf War was fought to defend it. Much of America's military planning in the region is geared at deterring or repelling future threats to Saudi Arabia—and, more specifically, to Saudi Arabian oil. To be sure, the nature of the Saudi regime is discomforting to many. Critics condemn a deficiency of democratic norms. Foreign policy experts believe that as a quid pro quo for our strategic umbrella, Saudi Arabia should be expected to openly advance U.S. interests in the Middle East. By contrast, the Saudi attitude has traditionally been one of keeping a low profile, occasionally supporting U.S. positions privately, but rarely in public. Beyond that, there are few examples of the regime pursuing an overtly "Saudi" foreign policy.

Conventional wisdom is overwhelmingly of the opinion that this cautious, low-keyed, even self-effacing stance will continue indefinitely. Lastly, there is a disconnect between the uninformed view of Saudi Arabia as a rich oil baron for whom money is no object and the reality of a Saudi Arabia that has been struggling with relatively low oil prices, sizable budgetary deficits, and nagging domestic economic problems for most of the past decade. Even professional economists and Wall Street analysts accept uncritically the proposition that Saudi Arabia will always favor oil price stability over high or rising prices.

Thus, in keeping with the objective of forcing simulation participants to think through the consequences of plot lines that diverge from conventional wisdom, the scenario described a quite different set of Saudi behaviors.

## The Story So Far . . .

Our starting point for the scenario was the simple recognition that the fictional global financial and economic crisis it spelled out would leave oil producers in a far stronger financial and economic position than they had enjoyed for many years. Given the improved position, Saudi behavior could also be expected to change substantially. "The Story So Far . . ." chronicled that change in some detail. With the outbreak of global financial turbulence, the Saudis signaled a generally more assertive and outward-looking posture by having the Saudi ambassador to Washington ask for a White House meeting to brief top officials on Saudi thinking on a number of topics. This is how the simulation participants were briefed on the Saudi ambassador's talking points in anticipation of that meeting:

> He explained that with the substantial rebound in oil prices Saudi Arabia was being given the opportunity to play a more activist role in the region. After a decade of periodic conflict, it wanted to explore new and unconventional ways of reducing tensions and possibly establishing greater stability. Accordingly, it was considering a number of departures, some quite bold.

First, it was thinking of building on the precedent of the Israeli-Syrian peace talks by offering Saddam Hussein the chance to rebuild peaceful relations. His government would be prepared to support ending all current and future U.N. economic sanctions in return for assurances that Iraq would agree to a nonaggression pact with Saudi Arabia.

Second, Saudi Arabia was exploring a parallel reconciliation initiative with Iran. As the initial step, it had drafted the terms of a technical cooperation agreement with Iran to secure shipping lanes in the Gulf.

Third, it was contemplating an indirect channel of communications with Israel to lay the foundation for a process of normalization following the successful completion of the Israeli-Syrian talks. Establishment of a Middle East humanitarian assistance fund, with contributions from all parties, could be proposed at a later stage.

Fourth, it was opening an indirect channel of communications with Islamic groups that have been critical of Saudi involvement with the U.S. military. This may eventually involve some changes in the facilities open to the United States.

As for its financial policy, the ambassador emphasized that Saudi dollar reserves are again more than adequate. Thus, the prudent course would be to sell U.S.-dollar denominated assets and diversify into assets denominated in the euro and yen.

## At the Simulation

Early in the simulation, participants were inundated by a flurry of reports that amplified aspects of the Saudi initiative. The Foreign Policy and National Security Group received several reports. They read that intelligence sources had learned that Saudi Arabia had decided to allow the smaller Gulf states to develop economic relations with Israel. The language Saudi officials used was along these lines: "While we do not intend to be out in front, we do not intend to stand in the way of any deals you reach." The group also found out that sources close to the adjourned investigation of the Kobar Towers bombing, in which nineteen American military personnel were killed, had told congressional staff that Saudi Arabia was aware of evidence indicating (but not conclusively proving) Iranian involvement. It was interested in Congress reopening the investigation to consider this evidence. The Foreign Policy and National Security Group was also made aware of a proposal by Venezuelan President Hugo Chávez to convene a special OPEC meeting to chart a new, more aggressive policy to enforce higher oil prices.

Meanwhile, both the Economics and Trade Group and the Central Banking Group were informed of a formal Saudi proposal to enable them to meet their objective of reallocating the currency composition of their official foreign exchange reserves. The Saudi financial authorities indicated that they would prefer achieving this diversification off-market, through a special private placement, in which the U.S. Treasury would create a new series of bonds similar to the Carter bonds of 1978–79. These would be bonds denominated in foreign currencies, such as the euro, the British pound sterling, and the Japanese yen. In other words, the U.S. government would be borrowing from Saudi Arabia not in its own currency, the U.S. dollar, but in a foreign currency, and thus it would take the risk of loss should the dollar depreciate against some or all of those currencies. The simulation participants were asked what counterproposal should be recommended to soothe Saudi concern about their own exposure to foreign exchange risk now that the dollar was coming under pressure in the world's foreign exchange markets.

## Tackling the Policy Problems

To the Decision-Makers Group, it was important to get a quick assessment of the change in Saudi attitudes. Were the ambassador's talking points for the White House meeting credible? Were the Saudis likely to follow through on any of the unprecedented courses of action? And most important, should the United States try to encourage or discourage them?

On the matter of a special financial facility to enable the Saudis to shift an unspecified portion of the country's reserves from dollars to other currencies, the experts were opposed to an off-market private placement. The Economics and Trade Group recognized the significance of the problem, given the amount of money involved, and the potential for large-scale Saudi sales of dollar assets to exacerbate U.S. economic problems by further depressing the value of the dollar. But they believed the best strategy was to persuade the Saudi government that it was in Saudi Arabia's own interest to preserve the value of the dollar—and hence the value of its existing prodigious holdings of financial assets denominated in dollars—and that the contemplated action would greatly weaken it. The Central Banking Group independently came up with the same recommendation.

However, there was some disagreement between the Foreign Policy and National Security Group and the Decision-Makers Group on how seriously to take the Saudi Arabian political initiatives. The Foreign Policy and National Security Group members were inclined to think that the laundry list of proposed actions was not credible and that the various components were inconsistent. The discussion within the group stressed that "the ambassador's talking points don't make sense . . . we need to find out what is really going on." They doubted that the Saudi government would follow through. They urged a stern response that reminded the Saudis of our close and long-standing security relationship and mutual interest in maintaining high oil production. What they felt was most important was to consider the broader national interest in promoting higher oil production among our allies, but also to use the Saudi opening as a way to explore better relations with Iran.

## Outcome

The developments in the Middle East, not only the Saudi initiatives but also the events that were playing out in Turkey (described in Chapter VIII), caused considerable concern among the members of the Decision-Makers Group. Their reaction was to go considerably further than the Foreign Policy and National

Security Group in demonstrating U.S. disapproval of much of what the Saudi ambassador was presenting. The secretary of defense, played by former Director of Central Intelligence James Woolsey, explained the group's reasoning along the following lines in the mid-day "press conference":

> When you put together the Saudi cooperation with Iran and Iraq—admittedly, in the scenario, tied in some way to their wanting to get along better with Israel—with the increase in the oil prices and the very clear threat to move some of our forces out of the Persian Gulf because of pressure from Islamic extremist groups in Saudi Arabia, we felt that threats to our anchors in both Turkey and Saudi Arabia were sufficiently substantial, and we had to take some rather firm action. We sent an aircraft carrier battle group to the Persian Gulf. The vice-chairman of the Joint Chiefs, a senior Treasury Department official, and the director of the CIA were asked to go quietly to investigate the Saudi request that some U.S. forces leave. The objective was to tell them in no way did we expect them to start cozying up to Iraqis and Iranians or to cut back on our presence in the Gulf. I believe we released some oil from the strategic petroleum reserve and told the Saudis we might well release more to stabilize the oil market. If you compare this to the more cooperative stance we took with Turkey, you would conclude it was a firm elbow in the ribs to the Saudis and a friendly embrace to the Turks.

The Foreign Policy and National Security Group acquiesced and formally agreed with these plans. But they urged a more diplomatic tone to the interchange. They felt that the delegation's primary purpose should be to lower oil prices by convincing the Saudis to increase production. They also suggested reminding the Saudis that the Venezuelan gambit for coopting OPEC is a common problem both for the United States and for Saudi Arabia, and that "we are prepared to work together in our security relationship and mutual partnership to solve the problem." They also reemphasized the need for the president to encourage all U.S. allies to increase oil production "so as to preempt Iran and Iraq from capturing gains" in the market.

## The Control Room Perspective

In preparing the scenario and the supplementary information that was revealed during the simulation itself, we were frequently asking ourselves (and knowledgeable colleagues at the Council) what lessons Saudi Arabia itself had taken from the economic and financial history of the past thirty years. Presumably, the Saudi leadership would try to avoid repeating what they viewed as mistakes—failing to diversify their holdings of marketable securities across the major currencies or increasing government spending programs to such an extent that they were in danger of amassing sizable budgetary deficits when oil prices declined—and would try to reapply successful strategies. But the United States had learned some lessons, as well. The simulation showed that U.S. officials and experts are not inclined to tolerate policy courses that suggest weakness or vulnerability, especially those that remind foreign governments and financial market participants about the "bad old days" of the 1970s, when worldwide inflation soared and investors incurred substantial real (i.e., inflation-adjusted) losses in their holdings of stocks and bonds.

# Chapter V

# Brazilian Financial Challenge: Discriminatory Treatment against U.S. Interests

## Real-World Backdrop

Brazil suffered a serious setback in the wake of the Russian debt default starting in the late summer of 1998. The Brazilian government tried to head off a major assault on the currency by announcing a package of strong fiscal measures, but it was undermined when the governor of one of Brazil's states declared that he would cease paying provincial debts owed to the central government. This blatant assault on the authority of the central government set off alarm bells throughout the financial markets; within days, Brazil was forced to let the currency float to avert a massive hemorrhaging of official reserves. World confidence was not immediately restored, although the appointment of Arminio Fraga, an economist who had gained considerable market experience working for Soros Fund Management in New York, had a significant positive effect. Gradually, market attitudes toward Brazilian prospects began to improve and the country appeared to be on the verge of resuming satisfactory rates of economic growth.

## The Story So Far . . .

The scenario cast doubts on Brazilian financial stability. After the outbreak of major new financial convulsions, "The Story So Far . . ." reported the following:

> Brazil was bombarded by substantial outflows of funds, including substantial capital flight by Brazilian corporations and wealthy individuals as well as foreign investors. With the currency falling sharply in the foreign exchange markets and therefore threatening to undermine recent progress toward curbing inflation, the Brazilian authorities sought to control the damage. But moderate-sized intervention in the foreign exchange market by the central bank had little effect in stemming the depreciation.

The unsuccessful intervention quickly triggered large-scale outflows of funds from Brazil to other markets, particularly Japan and Europe. Brazilian officials thus were facing a familiar, though no less agonizing, dilemma. They could attempt to service official debts in full, but in so doing they would almost certainly further deplete already diminished levels of official foreign exchange reserves. Or they could seek agreement from international holders of Brazilian bonds denominated in dollars to provide interest rate relief and other debt-amortization concessions.

## At the Simulation

Shortly after the simulation began, as participants were already struggling with how to stabilize American financial markets and deal with a half-dozen other fast breaking side-effects of the financial crisis, the simulation groups read the following email that outlined the fictional Brazilian government response to the unfolding crisis:

In the deteriorating market situation and to conserve foreign currency reserves for future requirements, Brazil has announced that
it could no longer continue to service in full its official hard
currency-denominated debt. Trading in secondary markets for
emerging country debt has seized up worldwide. American creditors have rejected the unilateral payments moratorium, which
they believe is illegal, and Brazil has refused to make scheduled
payments to U.S. bondholders. However, European, Japanese,
and other Asian creditors have agreed to provide an emergency
line of credit in return for partial servicing of the outstanding debt.
They believe that their regulators will judge this to be sufficient to
avoid reclassification of the credits. This discriminatory treatment
was rebuked by American financial institutions and by several
members of Congress briefed on the Brazilian action. A prominent
member of Congress from Arizona has threatened to introduce
legislation to sanction Brazil for this discriminatory behavior.

   Simulation participants also learned that the news of the Brazilian partial moratorium had a severe impact on U.S. institutions
with exposures to Brazil. U.S. stock prices were hit hard by
fears that other indebted countries might try to emulate the
Brazilian action.
   The questions for U.S. policymakers coursed across their computer screens in the form of email messages. The Decision-
Makers Group was asked generally to consider what should be
done about the Brazilian discriminatory behavior. The Economics and Trade Group was asked what the U.S. government should
do in support of U.S. creditors in Brazil. The Central Banking
Group was asked what role the Federal Reserve should play in
reaching a satisfactory resolution of Brazil's debt moratorium.
Finally, the Financial Regulatory Group was asked whether the
Brazilian action should be treated as a material event for the
American financial institutions that held the defaulted bonds,
and if so, how should those institutions be disclosing their potential losses and accounting for them?

## Tackling the Policy Problems

As participants became aware of the potential for setting dangerous precedents, the events precipitated a flurry of activity among simulation participants in each of the groups. The Financial Regulators acted first, affirming that a debt moratorium would have to be treated as a material event and that strict accounting standards would have to be applied. Later, they were pressed by the Economics and Trade Group. "On the issue of Brazil's default, the European and Japanese creditors have agreed to provide emergency lines of credit for partial servicing of debt because they believe their regulators will not classify the loans." They went on to ask, "Will our regulators give the U.S. banks similar treatment, i.e., give them the same benefit of the doubt?" The Financial Regulators replied: "We are expecting that a large amount of Brazilian loans will be classified. We expressed our concern to our foreign counterparts about the policy they are following. A coordinated response is highly preferable. But the specific answer to your question is 'No.'" As rapporteur Melvin Williams pointed out, "The group thought Financial Accounting Standards Board [FASB] rules should apply in order to avoid the creative accounting that would likely result from the emergency lines of credit." The bottom line: American accounting and disclosure standards are tough and would not be watered down by this group of experienced professionals.

Meanwhile, the Central Bankers, acknowledging the intrinsically international dimension, called for an immediate meeting of G-7 members, including the new European Central Bank as well as the Bank of Japan, to discuss the potential impact on the global financial system. But they also let the Decision-Makers Group know that they did not view the provocation as intrinsically a central banking problem, but that broader policy issues were also at stake.

The Economics and Trade Group also took the provocation extremely seriously. They emailed the Decision-Makers Group as follows: "If there is going to be a further default, we need first to try to avoid it or at least work in an orderly fashion. The U.S. government will have to play an active role in Brazil. There needs to be a common approach with the other G-7 countries to find a restructuring and ongoing system for Brazil that will meet some of each country's concerns. This is similar to what happened in the previous Latin American debt crises." Nick Beim, the rapporteur for the group, recounted his group's reasoning:

> Our primary concern was to restore multilateral coordination with Europe and Japan. Opinions differed as to how forceful we should be in our response to the European and Japanese repayment deal. Some favored condemnation of the deal, but most felt we should be constructive given that the deal had already been struck, and that—pending advice from regulators—we should try to persuade domestic creditors to accept the same partial repayment deal as had been given to Japanese and European creditors. We also felt we should send a strong signal to Europe and Japan that we would expect them to work more closely with us to help address the global economic crisis, and that their behavior in Brazil was not a constructive step in that direction. More broadly, we favored actively working with Europe and Japan to help restore Brazil's financial condition.

For its part, the Decision-Makers Group polled the Foreign Policy and National Security Group for its views on the impact of any anti-Brazilian legislation in the Congress. "If Congress debates and passes in subcommittee a bill taking control of Brazilian assets in the United States, would this further inflame matters or lead to substantive discussions with the Brazilians?" The Foreign Policy and National Security Group reported back that the first priority would be to try to dissuade Congress from doing this, explaining that the administration should apply political pressure instead. But group members warned that the president should be prepared to veto any such legislation.

The policy problem was deemed of critical importance by both the secretary of state and the secretary of the treasury. It was also personally annoying: America considered itself a friend of Brazil and has been a steadfast supporter through Brazil's many financial difficulties over the years. U.S. officials questioned why, all of a sudden, Brazil should be discriminating against American interests. They felt that reasonable people should be able to negotiate responsible compromises, and they were not doing that.

Here is how the Treasury secretary briefed the simulation participants in the middle of the controversy:

> On the Brazil side, the issue there is a lot more troubling, and we actually not only had meetings with the G-7 about the situation in Brazil, but also with the Brazilian finance minister, Pedro Malan.* The issue is that Brazil, once again, is in the middle of a crisis. That it has been brought on by contagion from all the other things that have been happening in the world is certainly part of the problem. They've taken the position that the U.S. banks, insurance companies, mutual funds, and hedge funds have all acted in concert to go up against Brazil and have decided not to accept any reductions in amounts due. Brazil is obviously in a bad way. They've spent a lot of money trying to hold up their currency, so they've lost a lot of reserves. Their economy is tanking, as is their stock market, and they need help. Their view is that the U.S. banks and other U.S. financial institutions just have not been sympathetic to Brazil's plight. The Europeans, on the other hand, have been sympathetic and have been willing to cut their loans and advance the desperately needed new funds, as have the Japanese. So, the Brazilians decided that they can selectively have a moratorium on the U.S. institutions and not on these other countries' institutions. That, of course, was unacceptable to the U.S. government.
>
> We went first to the G-7 to see if we could rally support to reject out of hand this discriminatory approach that Brazil seems to have taken. But the G-7 basically let us know that they weren't

---

* In reality, the secretaries of state and treasury went to the Control Room and conducted a mock telephone call with the Brazilian minister. To keep the already complex simulation from getting too complicated, the Control Room played the role of foreign officials for all discussions and negotiations.

interested in cooperating with the United States on this, that somehow or another we got ourselves into this problem. In a way, in side comments in the hallways, you heard them talking, "Well it's about time the U.S. banks got what was coming to them." So, we've got some work to do with the G-7 on the issue of Brazil.

Talking with the Brazilian minister himself, which was a very interesting exercise, we learned that the Brazilian foreign ministry took the position that there was a conspiracy among U.S. institutions. We told him that we have seen no evidence of that at Treasury, but we promised to at least look into the issue. It was clear that the Brazilians see a conspiracy and an attempt to be high-handed, in what they regard to be typical U.S. fashion with regard to Brazil.

We sat down and told them their policy action was very counterproductive, that if we ever got into a situation where countries are played off each other as a basis for getting paid back, it is unlikely that the United States would enter again into loans of this kind with emerging markets. They said, "Yes, fine, well and good, but Europe and Japan are playing along and what we really think is that the U.S. banks and institutions should come back to the bargaining table and negotiate." We then said, "Look, we understand. From the point of view of Treasury, we think it's unfortunate and bad policy. However, there is a movement afoot in Congress, and a bill is about to be presented, which would have the effect of seizing all Brazilian assets in the United States in retaliation for the selective default." The representatives of the Brazilian Ministry got on the phone, talked directly to Malan, and Malan got back to us immediately and said, "Well, it just so happens that we have been studying the amount of U.S. investment in Brazil. And there's a lot of multinational U.S. investment in Brazil, so if you do take that step, which we also would find unfortunate, don't think we are without our recourses."

They then again said, "If you are willing, see if you can get the U.S. financial institutions to come back to the bargaining table in some way. Then we would be willing to hold off on the moratorium and not cut any separate side deals." That's how it's been left so far. That is a decision that is pending back with the Decision-Makers Group.

The secretary of state added an additional comment to this comprehensive briefing on the delicate situation and the policy dilemma it created:

> We were sure that we needed to talk with our friends and allies and the larger powers around the world before we reacted. We tried to enlist the support of other banks around the world to take our side and to not let U.S. financial institutions and the U.S. government be put in a subordinated position by Brazil in the repayment of their loans. But we were unsuccessful. They were unwilling to do that. So, we tried to keep the issue alive by saying that we would find other forums for discussing the issue. It was a large matter of principle, in our opinion, that it would set a very bad precedent to allow a bankrupt country to prioritize their own loan repayment. We thought that it would be disruptive to both financial and political stability in the world. We couldn't allow that precedent to be established.

## Outcome

Within the context of the simulation, because these officials made a conscientious effort to understand the motivations and the negotiating positions of the Brazilian officials, they were able to avoid unilateral actions that would have proved unwieldy, if not impossible, to unwind at a later point. During the second half of the simulation, the decision-makers were told that the CEO of a major U.S. bank heavily involved in Latin America had requested a conversation with the U.S. Treasury secretary with respect to the proposed Brazilian moratorium. Eventually this meeting was held and provided a face-saving route to getting the American financial institutions back into negotiations with the Brazilians. A coordinated program to stretch out interest payments and an arrangement for new credits was agreed to by all major creditors.

## The Control Room Perspective

In drafting the scenario, we thought that if there were ever actually a "rebellion" against American triumphalism, one of the ways it would surface would be through an attempt at overt discrimination against American interests, whether in the areas of trade or finance, or in another aspect of international relations. Such discrimination is rare these days, but was surely not unknown in other eras, before multilateral institutions such as the IMF and World Bank were established to prevent it.

The Brazil plot line was thus designed. The decision-makers came to realize the potential importance of this fictional development because of the power of such a rebellion to set a precedent and perhaps induce other countries also to discriminate against U.S. interests. But the group's personal involvement and interest in the conflict was surely roused by the attitude of the fictional Brazilians. The Brazilians were calm. They knew their position. They were almost apologetic, more regretful than angered by their belief that the U.S. financial institutions were conspiring against them. They also knew the real world U.S. policy position as expressed by top U.S. Treasury officials on behalf of the Clinton administration: namely, that at times of financial duress for a heavily indebted country, private-sector lenders should share the burden and be prepared to take a hit. The fictional Brazilian officials would use that position as partial justification for their course of action. They also fully anticipated that initially they would be threatened with sanctions, but they felt confident they could head off sanctions by calling attention to the leverage they could exert over the operations of U.S. multinational corporations in Brazil.

By the end of the simulation, the obdurate U.S. creditors eventually backed down and asked the U.S. authorities to mediate a resumption of discussions between them and the Brazilian Finance Ministry. Thus, the hard-nosed Brazilian strategy achieved a positive result. Other countries might well have concluded that discriminatory treatment can work if it can be made to appear reasonable or justifiable to U.S. government officials.

# Chapter VI

# Argentina: Currency Board in Jeopardy

## Real-World Backdrop

Argentina, after years of ineffective monetary policy, rampant inflation, and economic decline, adopted a currency board–like system in 1991. Here are some of the key elements of that system:[1]

- A currency board is a monetary authority that issues notes and coins convertible into a foreign anchor currency (for Argentina, the U.S. dollar) or commodity at a truly fixed rate and on demand.

- As reserves, a currency board holds low-risk, interest-bearing bonds and other assets denominated in the anchor currency, for instance U.S. Treasury bills.

- An orthodox currency board has no discretion in monetary policy. Its operations are completely passive and automatic; market forces alone determine the money supply.

- Unlike a central bank, an orthodox currency board does not lend to the domestic government, to domestic companies, or to domestic banks. In a currency board system, the government can finance its spending by only taxing or borrowing, not by printing money and thereby creating inflation.

- Interest rates and inflation: An orthodox currency board does not try to influence interest rates like a typical central bank. The fixed exchange rate with the anchor currency encourages arbitrage that tends to keep interest rates and inflation in the currency board country roughly the same as those in the anchor-currency country.

- A currency board has no responsibility for acting as a lender of last resort to protect domestic banks from losses.

- Argentina's system is not an orthodox currency board, but a currency board–*like* system because its central bank retains many of its old powers, but is constrained by currency board rules regarding the exchange rate and reserves.

- The potential problem with currency board–like systems is that they have loopholes that allow the central banks considerable discretionary power, power that a pure currency board is intended to dilute.

- In Argentina, the minimum foreign reserve ratio is not 100 percent, as it is for an orthodox currency board, but 66 percent. Though the actual foreign reserve ratio hovers around 90 percent, the legal freedom the central bank has to reduce foreign reserves has at times created speculative attacks on the currency. People have been afraid that reducing foreign reserves toward the legal minimum would be the first step in a chain of events that would return Argentina to the previous (failed) central banking system.

The Argentine currency board system has not been a panacea for Argentina. The Brazilian financial crisis of 1998 and subsequent devaluation left Argentine industry at a severe competitive disadvantage, and Argentina suffered a significant, long-lasting business downturn. Foreign investors had already been shunning existing dollar-denominated bonds of the Argentine government, with yields ranging as much as 10 percentage points above comparable U.S. Treasury securities. Market participants have been unconvinced that the Argentine version of a currency board can be successfully sustained.

The U.S. government's official position on international monetary arrangements has evolved over time. By the end of the Clinton administration, after witnessing many countries' bad experiences during the repeated financial disturbances of the mid- to late 1990s, the policy was generally to discourage countries from adopting fixed exchange rates or even crawling peg mechanisms, in which a fixed exchange rate is allowed to depreciate at a predetermined pace. These experiences proved that hardly any developing country has sufficient official foreign exchange reserves or access to global credit markets to fend off a speculative attack on its currency in the midst of a crisis. And the large-scale currency devaluations that usually follow the abandonment of a currency peg are highly disruptive—to the domestic banking system, to the financial positions of companies that borrowed in foreign currencies, and to the government's own credibility. Some form of managed floating exchange rate is viewed as a better choice.

However, the U.S. government has not been entirely opposed to currency board–type monetary arrangements. It has applauded the Hong Kong version, and it has been mildly supportive of Argentina's, acknowledging that the country has avoided replicating past bouts with hyperinflation since moving to a currency board–like system. So far, the Bush administration has taken no early steps to reverse or even modify this stance.

## The Story So Far . . .

The scenario described how the global financial crisis spilled over onto Argentina:

> The repercussions of renewed financial volatility in Brazil and in the emerging debt markets were felt most urgently in Argentina.

While the Argentine peso, tied to the U.S. dollar through its currency board, was dropping along with the dollar against the euro and the Japanese yen, it was surging against the Brazilian real. To many Argentines, the outcome represented the worst of both worlds—large outflows of capital from Argentina combined with an appreciation against the currency of its most important trading partner.

## At the Simulation

Simulation participants received this information shortly after the game began:

> With Argentina faced with continuing outflows of capital that were quickly draining its external dollar reserves, to buy time Argentine officials decided to request establishment of a new contingency financing facility, including a large swap line with the Federal Reserve and access to the U.S. Treasury's Exchange Stabilization Fund. The Argentine finance minister offered his assessment that without the facility, which he envisaged would eventually be buttressed by additional IMF support, Argentina might have to abandon the currency board and allow the peso to float freely. It was his view that this would trigger a new round of chaos throughout the region that might go beyond the financial and encompass the economic and political dimensions as well.

Both the Economics and Trade Group and the Central Banking Group were asked for their policy recommendations on how the United States should respond.

The Economics and Trade Group discussed this problem at some length. There was debate as to whether Argentina had a special claim on U.S. financial assistance because of its currency board. Some believed that they did, given the potential impact that serious financial problems in Argentina might have on the U.S. economy. Others disagreed, viewing the potential economic impact on the United States as minimal. Most agreed, however, that any solution for Argentina should have a Brazilian component given the tight linkages between the two countries and the concurrent Brazilian crisis.

The Central Banking Group took quite a different message from its deliberations. Early in the simulation, the central bankers decided that the United States response should be subordinated to the views of the IMF. After all, Argentina had an IMF program in place and any multilateral financing on top of those resources would have to be integrated into the existing program. Later they learned that the Economics and Trade Group was seriously considering providing support to Argentina unilaterally—outside an IMF-led initiative. To forestall such a move, the central bankers sent an emissary to the Economics and Trade Group to make clear that Federal Reserve money would not be forthcoming if support for Argentina was undertaken unilaterally rather than in connection with an IMF-led program.

In the end, the Economics and Trade Group came around to the position that any financial assistance to the countries should be multilateral, not U.S.-based. So the group's final policy recommendation was to offer financial assistance to both Argentina and Brazil, contingent on both countries adopting specific financial policies that would help stabilize their economies. And both groups concurred in a recommendation that the United States should work with other G-7 countries to stabilize both economies.

## The Control Room Perspective

The Argentine problem posed a close call, with reasonable arguments on both sides. The IMF-multilateral approach that was chosen was well grounded in precedent and in logic. But if the Decision-Makers Group had given the Argentine plight a high priority and wished to run a more interdependent relationship with South America, it might have insisted on a U.S.-led package. Would the Central Banking Group have resisted a direct request from the White House for a swap line with Argentina? Maybe not, but it would have led to an interesting series of interchanges between an independent central bank and a proactive executive branch.

It is instructive to reflect on what actually happened in Argentina just ten months after the January 2000 simulation. The capital flight feared by the fictional Argentine government did in fact develop. A number of adverse economic and political developments raised doubts in the minds of many investors, domestic and foreign alike, about the ability of Argentina to service its huge foreign-currency debt of over $140 billion, or 50 percent of the country's GDP. In the ensuing rush out of Argentine peso assets and into U.S. dollars, the currency board was strained almost to the breaking point.

Faced with a massive loss of foreign currency reserves and an abrupt loss of confidence, the Argentine government had no choice but to seek financial assistance. As in the simulation, requests for bilateral financing were turned aside, and Argentina was compelled to go back to the IMF to assemble a new funding package. By the time all the pieces of that package were complete, it totaled some $40 billion (although market experts put the figure of actual new financial resources made available at a much lower amount). Drawings on the expanded IMF facility were conditioned on Argentina meeting stern conditions, especially on the size and composition of its government budget deficit. But the ability to gain legislative support for what were bound to be highly unpopular measures proved to be inadequate. Within the space of three weeks in March 2001, two successive economics ministers, José Luis Machinea and Ricardo López Murphy, resigned when their plans could not be ratified by the Argentine Congress. The third economics "czar," Domingo Cavallo, the original architect of Argentina's anti-inflation policy in the early 1990s and founder of the currency board, took over amidst considerable concern over his ability to convince recalcitrant legislators to approve painful budget cuts. Not surprisingly, Argentine financial markets remained exceptionally volatile during those fitful weeks. A number of market participants feared that if Cavallo failed to quell the domestic political opposition to the strong budgetary reforms essential for accessing the multilateral financing package, the Argentine government might choose to default on existing bonds.

To the contrary, in June 2001, Argentina secured sufficient market support to undertake a multi-billion dollar swap of existing obligations for longer-term bonds in order to stretch out debt servicing requirements. However, the rate of interest that was needed to induce bondholders to take part in the swap was extremely high—almost ten percentage points above interest rates of comparable U.S. government securities. This signified persisting concern over the ultimate resolution of Argentina's financial difficulties.

## Notes

1.  Kurt Schuler and Steve H. Hanke, *Currency Boards for Developing Countries: A Handbook* (San Francisco: ICS Press, 1994).

# Chapter VII

# Financial Market Fallout: SIPC Cash Crunch

### Real-World Backdrop

Ask the next hundred people walking down Main Street or Fifth Avenue who protects their deposits if their bank goes bust and chances are pretty good that a sizable number will correctly answer "the federal government." Many may actually be able to pin it down further: "the FDIC" (Federal Deposit Insurance Corporation). But ask a hundred investors who protects the stocks they own if their broker goes under, and the replies will be all over the map. Some will also cite the federal government, many will (incorrectly) say the New York Stock Exchange or NASD, but the overwhelming majority will admit they don't have the foggiest idea. In fact, there is ample evidence that public awareness of the existence of the Securities Industry Protection Corporation (SIPC) is practically nil.[1] But that's the correct answer.

To get a sense of the importance of that institution and why simulation participants thought long and hard about the policy significance of questions about its financial viability, a brief profile of SIPC is worthwhile. The information below is drawn from SIPC's website.[2]

1. *What is SIPC's basic protection?*

   SIPC protects securities customers of member broker-dealers. If a member fails financially, SIPC may ask a federal court to appoint a trustee to liquidate the firm and protect its customers, or, in limited situations involving smaller firms, SIPC may protect the customers directly. Each customer is protected up to a maximum of $500,000 for securities and up to $100,000 on claims for cash.

2. *Does SIPC protect mutual funds or money market funds when they are held in accounts with SIPC members?*

   Yes, because shares of mutual funds are securities and are protected in the same manner as traditional securities like stocks and bonds.

3. *Who are the members of SIPC?*

   Just about every broker-dealer operating in the United States. That includes discount brokers and the new electronic brokers.

4. *Where does SIPC get its money?*

   The money required to protect customers beyond that which is available from the property in the possession of the failed broker-dealer is advanced by SIPC from a fund maintained for that purpose. The sources of money for the SIPC Fund are assessments collected from SIPC members and interest on investments in U.S. government securities.

5. *What if these resources are insufficient?*

   In an emergency, SIPC may borrow up to $1 billion from the U.S. Treasury through the Securities and Exchange Commission (SEC) if the SEC determines such a loan is necessary to protect customers and maintain confidence in U.S. securities markets.

6. *Who runs SIPC?*

   SIPC is governed by a Board of Directors consisting of seven members. Five are appointed by the president of the United States (subject to Senate confirmation), of whom two are representatives of the general public and three, the securities industry. In addition, one member each is designated by the secretary of the treasury and the Federal Reserve Board from among their officials.

## At the Simulation

The SIPC policy problem was not revealed in "The Story So Far . . . ." But there were hints that the severity of the stock market break in the United States was capable of unleashing strong adverse consequences on various elements of the financial system. Banks would be reluctant to provide additional credit to security firms unless they were certain that they were solvent and would remain so. Mutual funds were faced with the prospect of substantial redemptions by their investors and had to prepare for the worst-case scenario by taking steps to improve their liquidity.

In the final stages of the simulation, members of three groups—Financial Regulatory, Central Banking, and Economics and Trade—received the following message from the White House staff:

> The explosion of electronic trading of securities and the subsequent decline in market values have resulted in large claims against online brokers unable to complete transactions in a timely manner. This has led to the failure of some of them. Affected customers have filed for compensation from SIPC. Payment of such claims would leave SIPC significantly underfunded. In addition, online brokers have reportedly mishandled margin debt and appear to be in violation of Federal Reserve regulations.

The members of the expert groups were asked what should be done to shore up the financial condition of SIPC and what initiatives were needed to improve regulation of electronic trading of securities.

## Tackling the Policy Problems

These were problems that cut across the institutional responsibilities of the three expert groups involved. [That is as true in the real world as it was in the simulation.] Not surprisingly, it was the Financial Regulatory Group, which was constructed to be a composite of all of the major official institutions involved in supervising and regulating financial institutions and markets other than the Federal Reserve, that immediately took the lead. The group's spirited internal debate spanned both narrow technical issues and broader policy issues where decisions would inevitably be precedent-setting. They dealt with traditional questions of how to maintain an orderly flow of credit to troubled institutions from their bankers while moving expeditiously to close down insolvent organizations. It was those failures that would then lead to claims on SIPC financial resources. They also had to keep an eye on the issue of how to maintain the viability of the fastest growing segment of the marketplace—i.e., electronic trading mechanisms. The group was aware that the policy problem also involved assessing the impact of failed trades on mutual funds, and the ability of mutual funds to conduct their business in rapidly moving markets.

For the Financial Regulators, coming to a consensus on what to do turned out to be difficult. The members of the group virtually split down the middle on their analysis of the issues, and their ultimate recommendations reflected a series of compromises and accommodations to opposing factions. Proponents of securing additional financial support for SIPC noted that SIPC already has the statutory authority to draw on a billion-dollar credit line with the U.S. Treasury by going through the SEC. They argued that those funds could be activated quickly.

The real question the group wrestled with was what contingency plans to make on the assumption that failures of brokerage firms would be so widespread in the future that $1 billion would not be enough. Supporters of SIPC believed that it was essential to maintain the public's confidence that SIPC stood ready and was able to honor all potential claims. If it turned out more financial resources were necessary, Congress could provide those funds.

Others took a more Darwinian approach. They thought that, in the short term, customer accounts of the failing online brokerages should be transferred to more financially secure brokerages and that, only then should claims associated with those accounts be sorted out. For the medium to long term, instead of raising funds to shore up SIPC, either from the brokerage industry or from the taxpayer, these members favored eliminating SIPC altogether and replacing it with a system of private insurance. The unhappy experience with deposit insurance during the late 1980s and early 1990s obviously was on their minds.

The Financial Regulatory Group laid out its conclusions in the following recommendations:

1.  Customer accounts should first be transferred to solvent broker-dealers.
2.  SIPC claims must then be investigated to determine validity.
3.  If SIPC's available funding should prove insufficient to cover all legitimate claims, the group would advocate industry coverage of the excess.
4.  As a last resort, Congress must appropriate further funds.
5.  The Chairman of the SEC should set up a special commission comprised of representatives of government and industry to investigate alleged margin and other violations and report back within thirty days.

The Economics and Trade Group was concerned that any failure to support SIPC's ability to meet customer claims could lead to a crisis of confidence that would exacerbate the domestic economic crisis. They initially came up with a recommendation that pushed the burden of shoring up liquidity onto the Federal Reserve, rather than onto the Treasury. But their formal recommendation was similar to that of the financial regulators: "The administration should provide liquidity to SIPC to enable it to fund legitimate claims until SIPC gets its finances strong again. The administration should tie this aid to greater adherence to Federal Reserve margin requirements on the part of the online brokerage firms."

Having made the recommendation that SIPC receive additional funds, the Financial Regulatory Group's attention turned to how to prevent a credit crunch for the brokerage industry if the commercial banks on which they depended for day-to-day liquidity were to panic. One faction of the group suggested that the Fed should make a general speech to calm the markets— and the banks—and encourage banks to maintain normal credit relationships.[3] Another faction held out for a tougher line, even if it meant closing down banks that had overlent to the stock market, or suspending mutual fund redemptions.

The group coalesced around the idea of a special program for mutual funds to fend off any crisis precipitated by a large level of fund redemptions. This suggestion was sent to the Central Banking Group, which was initially unresponsive until informed by the regulators that the OCC and FDIC had determined that a number of banks were insolvent and needed to be closed.

The central bankers supported the concept after more complete explanation of its rationale.


## The Control Room Perspective

The United States is ahead of other advanced industrial countries in making the transition from a financial system based on traditional commercial banks to one in which the open capital markets play the central role. A well-developed private pension fund system, a tremendously inventive and technically competent mutual fund industry, sophisticated risk-management techniques, and a broad-based equity culture are distinctive elements in this transition.

That is not to say that the government does not play an important role, too. While most people give lip service to a philosophy
of deregulation and tolerance of market innovation (and to
change in principle), those with a practical outlook are reluctant
to force institutions to knuckle under to the undiluted discipline
of the marketplace. Market participants may grouse about the
complexity and often duplicative official supervisory and regulatory structure that characterize the American approach. But
when the chips are down, the safety nets that are embedded in
this structure are not easily discarded. The simulation participants were confronted with a hypothetical shock to the financial
stability of perhaps the least known of those safety nets. They
considered going the route of untrammeled market discipline.
But in the end they stopped short and worked within the current,
messy, but broadly successful system instead.

## Notes

1.  See Pamela Yip, "How Financial Is Your IQ?" *Houston Chronicle,*
    Business 1, November 4, 1996; and Kathy M. Kristof, "Investment
    Illiteracy: Survey Shows Public Lacks Basic Financial Knowledge,"
    *Austin American-Statesman,* sec. E2, May 26, 1996.

2.  http://www.sipc.org/publications/index.html

3.  This was along the lines of speeches that Federal Reserve Chair
    Greenspan made during previous financial disturbances. See Alan
    Greenspan, "Do Efficient Financial Markets Mitigate Financial Cri-
    ses?" Speech before the 1999 Financial Markets Conference of the
    Federal Reserve Bank of Atlanta, Sea Island, Georgia, October 19,
    1999; "The Federal Reserve's Semiannual Monetary Policy Report."
    Speech before the Committee on Banking, Housing, and Urban
    Affairs, U.S. Senate, July 21, 1998.

# Chapter VIII

# Turkey and Contagion: Multiple Loyalties

## Real-World Backdrop

Turkey is an important ally of the United States but is also dedicated to joining the European Union. Yet, Turkey's economic and financial circumstances have long diverged fundamentally from EU norms. During the 1997–98 global financial turmoil, the Turkish economy was a conspicuous casualty. GDP and industrial production both fell by close to 5 percent, while personal consumption dropped by nearly 7 percent in real, inflation-adjusted terms. The biggest problems Turkey faced were monetary and financial in character. Whereas Western Europe was bringing inflation down to negligible rates, Turkey had spent most of the 1990s in the Brazilian league, with near triple-digit inflation. Even in the midst of a business recession, consumer prices were rising by close to 65 percent per year by late 1999. While European governments were imposing strict austerity in order to meet the Maastricht regulations that required the annual government deficit to remain below 3 percent of GDP for admission to the common currency (the euro), Turkey's public sector deficit had remained in the neighborhood of 10 percent of

GDP. The government was heavily dependent on inflows of short-term capital from abroad to finance the deficit, requiring extraordinarily high interest rates. In this difficult economic environment, the credit rating agencies ranked Turkish public sector debt as among the five riskiest in the world.

Recognizing the economic and financial predicament, the new Turkish government formed after the April 1999 elections embarked on a policy course aimed at dealing with the chronic inflation problem, including fiscal, monetary, and structural reforms. The government also sought and attained a stand-by credit facility from the IMF to provide additional financial resources to backstop the program.

In their joint "letter of intent" to the IMF dated December 6, 1999, a month before our January 2000 simulation, Turkey's finance minister and central bank governor offered the following assessment:

> Over the last twenty-five years, inflation has weakened Turkey's economic performance in different ways. The most apparent is the instability of economic growth, as periods of rapid economic expansion have alternated with periods of equally rapid decline in economic activity. But the economic and social effects of inflation have been much more far-reaching. Growth has not only been volatile, but has also been well below the average of the most successful emerging markets. Higher growth rates must be sustained over time, if the existing income gap with respect to European Union (EU) countries is to be closed.
>
> By undermining confidence in the Turkish lira, inflation has also resulted in high and unstable nominal and real interest rates, with dramatic consequences for the society. Speculative and arbitrage activities have attracted more and more resources, and have distorted the working of financial markets and institutions. When the government has to pay on its debt real interest rates of 30 percent or more, private capital moves away from job-creating activities into financial investment. When banks have to charge even higher real interest rates on their loans, the credit process is disrupted and enterprises that have limited access to external

capital suffer. Moreover, these high real interest rates, together with a weak fiscal primary position, have pushed public finances onto an unsustainable path. This leaves Turkey vulnerable to swings in international financial markets' confidence.

The IMF had been optimistic that the process of bringing inflation down to Western standards would yield one-time benefits to Turkish banks and that the transition to a low-inflation economy would provide a foundation for greater stability of the banking system over the long run. What they avoided discussing is the question of what might happen to the Turkish banking system in the event that progress toward dealing with the inflation problem stalled or was reversed. But that is the hypothetical situation Turkey would encounter in the simulation.

Another important event took place just before the simulation: the European Union officially accepted Turkey's application as a formal candidate for EU membership. This has long been a highly controversial subject. Most European leaders take for granted that it will take many years for Turkey to measure up to the economic and financial standards required for membership. In private, though, the gesture is described as a less than firm commitment. Putting aside that cynical calculation, public opinion in many West European countries is deeply split, if not hostile, to Turkey joining the EU because of the implications it would have for heightened immigration of Turks seeking better job opportunities. At a time of high unemployment, this is no trivial consideration.

## The Story So Far . . .

The scenario painted a bleak financial picture for Turkey, complicated by several classical foreign policy incidents. The global financial crisis reopened incompletely healed wounds. The banking system fell into disarray. The central bank was buffeted with substantial capital outflows and spent heavily from its reserves in a vain attempt to shore up the Turkish lira. The recently adopted IMF program suddenly appeared unworkable.

In the political realm, Iran (in defiance of U.S. sanctions) was trying to reestablish economic and trade ties, much as it had been doing with the major West European nations. Human rights activists in the United States had shifted their focus from China to Turkey and were pressing for congressional legislation to restrict U.S. arms sales to Turkey and possibly limit trade relations. The Turkish government believed this to be totally unacceptable and privately threatened to restrict access to Incrlik Air Base in retaliation.

## Tackling the Policy Problems

The Turkey channel posed the single largest number of plot lines for any country in the fictional scenario. The simulation participants were asked to come to grips with some half-dozen problems: 1) What to do about the threat of failures among Turkey's banks; 2) Whether to put U.S. support behind a plan to water down Turkey's IMF program so that the country would not fall out of compliance and lose access to IMF funding; 3) How to deal with a bill in Congress to restrain trade with Turkey; 4) How to react to Iran's economic overture; 5) How to maintain access to Incrlik Air Base; and 6) What to do about the potential for Europe stalling on a timetable for Turkish membership in the European Union.

The discussions in the various groups generated a sophisticated appreciation of the complexity and difficulty of these policy problems and resulted in a firm consensus on many issues. In particular, every group was prepared to oppose and, if necessary, have the president veto any trade sanctions that might get pushed through the Congress by human rights groups, however well-meaning their motives.

The main economic and financial issues were debated extensively within the Economics and Trade Group, which judged that it was important to provide Turkey with financial assistance given its military and political relationship with the United States. Group members were acutely aware, however, that any action taken in Turkey would send signals to the rest of the world and establish precedents for dealing with other countries. Members of the group were also concerned with moral hazard issues and public relations problems that would result from a renegotiation of Turkey's IMF package. In other words, leniency might lead other countries to abandon painful economic policies on the notion that IMF or U.S. money would be made available to help them through their financial difficulties. Consequently, the Economics and Trade Group recommended that the U.S. government work with European countries to put together an emergency package that would support any additional funds that Turkey would need to repay IMF loans, discourage Turkey from taking risk exposures in the forward foreign exchange market, provide export credit facilities to Turkey via the U.S. Export-Import Bank, and not hold up emergency assistance in a financial crisis on human rights grounds.

The three groups that considered the options for the Turkish bank were unanimous in their analysis. They decided that the central bank of Turkey should be asked to step in and help with an orderly liquidation of the Turkish bank's contracts. But U.S. financial support for the bank was rejected. The Financial Regulatory Group felt that the Turkish banking crisis was for the IMF to handle, in conjunction with the relevant Turkish authorities. After all, the group reasoned, an IMF program was already in effect and maintaining banking system stability was part and parcel of the IMF's traditional role. The Central Banking Group, recognizing the deepening relationship between the EU and neighbors who aspired to become members, recommended leaving the Turkish banking crisis for the Europeans to work out with the Turkish government.

What about the traditional foreign policy dimension of the fictional Turkey plot line? The Foreign Policy and National Security Group was asked to consider virtually all aspects of the U.S. strategic relationship against the backdrop of serious economic, financial, and political troubles. It had to weigh in on the human rights issue, rejecting the use of trade sanctions. It had to respond to the Turkish threat to impede access to the Incrlik Air Base, recognizing that maintaining the Incrlik base was a crucial national interest and should not be used as a bargaining chip. It had to decide whether to push for Turkish EU membership, appreciating that whatever the United States said on this would probably have little influence on what the Europeans themselves decided.

Most controversially, the Foreign Policy and National Security Group also had to develop a strategy for responding to Iran's initiative to Turkey. This led to a wide-ranging discussion of the complex factors at work in U.S.-Iranian relations and allowed the group to open the door to make policy recommendations regarding Iran. The group was unanimously enthusiastic about using Turkey's opening of relations with Iran as a positive development in U.S. rapprochement with the Islamic republic.

The trouble was that the Decision-Makers Group saw things entirely differently. When the Foreign Policy and National Security Group made a recommendation to use the Turkish connection to begin a dialogue with Iran, the Decision-Makers responded acidly:

> President Mohammad Khatami's favorite founding father is Cotton Mather, not Thomas Jefferson, and in any case he cannot and has not checked substantial Iranian growth in use of terror and domestic suppression of reformers and democrats in recent Majlis elections. Your suggestion presupposes reforms that haven't yet occurred in Iran.

Yet, the Decision-Makers Group was prepared to go a long way to shore up the Turkish situation. To recapitulate what the secretary of defense told simulation participants, "With respect to the Turks, we dealt in a far more friendly fashion by essentially telling them that the president would veto the trade restrictions bill if it came through the Congress; that we were going to take the Turkish side with respect to EU entrance; and we expected, under those circumstances, for them to continue to permit our use of Incrlik and for their companies to taper down their dealings with the Iranians." In sum, it was a friendly embrace of the Turks.

## The Control Room Perspective

To participants in financial markets, Turkey has long been remarkable among developing countries. For years, it breached just about every tenet of U.S. economic policy first principles, but it was never taken to task. Internal political stability has been dubious as well. Now that Turkey is committed to bringing its economic and financial conditions in line with Western nations, any setback would be a source of considerable tension.

The fictional scenario was developed to test that proposition. It mixed conventional economic and financial policy elements with classical foreign policy and security themes, but with a slight twist: the country in question had divided loyalties. In the future, American policymakers will almost certainly have to analyze relations from the double perspective of dealing with a country bilaterally and dealing with that country as a European Union member—or aspirant. Plenty of European countries resist U.S. positions—take, for example, U.S. trade sanctions on Iran or Libya. Economic and financial ties between a country like Turkey—or Poland or soon Russia—and Western Europe are eventually going to be more important, intimate, and influential than ties with the United States. How far things have moved from the cases of the United Kingdom and Italy in the mid-1970s, when they faced financial pressures and had to go to the IMF for financial support. The United States had substantial influence over the evolution and implementation of those programs. Nowadays it would be far-fetched to think of any EU member going to the IMF for a similar financial program. Now if a country such as Italy had financial difficulties, it would be a matter for Italy and its fellow participants in the monetary union to sort out, all bound together by a common currency and an elaborate set of financing arrangements conditioned by formal undertakings consistent with Maastricht treaty obligations.*

Like Argentina, Turkey came under enormous pressure in late 2000 and early 2001, despite the existence of what looked on paper to be an admirable adjustment program worked out in coordination with the IMF. What went wrong? Turkey failed to move quickly and credibly to deal with the real-world banking problems hinted at in the fictional scenario. Both Turks and outsiders came to the conclusion that the Turkish government would be unable to keep the exchange rate within the prescribed path and that a significant devaluation would be unavoidable. The result was a rush to the exits by investors, a severe loss of foreign currency reserves, and an astonishing surge in interest rates on overnight deposits to over 4,000 percent per year at the worst of the crisis, some of the highest interest rates ever recorded. When the combination of currency support and the severe monetary squeeze was insufficient to restore investor confidence and induce reflows into the Turkish currency, the government was forced to devalue the lira and let it find its own level. It immediately sunk by nearly a third. Inevitable though that might have been, it jeopardized the entire policy framework that underlay the IMF program. It would arouse inflationary pressures, wreck the financial health of many highly indebted Turkish companies, and worsen the already precarious financial position of numerous Turkish banks.

In early 2001, Turkey looked to economist and World Bank vice president Kemal Dervis to take over as economic policy coordinator. The U.S. government pledged full support for the policy measures the new team was preparing, because in the end, Turkey was, and is, too important a strategically to be

---

* The Maastricht Treaty is defined as the "international agreement approved by the heads of government of the states of the European Community (EC) in Maastricht, Netherlands, in December 1991. It was ratified by all EC member states before November 1, 1993, when it came into force. The treaty established a European Union, with Union citizenship for every person holding nationality of a member state. It also provided for the introduction of a central banking system and a common currency, and it committed the EC nations to implementing a common foreign and security policy." Britannica.com.

allowed to fail economically and financially. But markets remained unconvinced that the necessary policy reforms could be effectively carried out in the face of repeated large-scale public demonstrations organized by opponents of the proposed budgetary cuts.

# Chapter IX

# Dangerous Contraband: Libya, Russia, and Stolen Nuclear Material

## Real-World Backdrop

Libya is among those states that have the capability and the motivation to develop weapons of mass destruction. For its part, Russia has a vast, aging, and not well-secured stockpile of nuclear weapons, parts, and supplies. It demonstrably has a level of lawlessness and corruption that justifies concern and vigilance over whether any of that material might fall into the wrong hands.

In 1996, President Clinton signed the Iran and Libya Sanctions Act (ILSA). As the White House explained at the time, the act imposes new sanctions on foreign companies that engage in specified economic transactions with Iran or Libya. Its stated purpose was to deny Iran and Libya revenues that could be used to finance international terrorism, limit the flow of resources necessary to obtain weapons of mass destruction, and put pressure on Libya to comply with U.N. resolutions that, among other things, called for Libya to extradite for trial the accused perpetrators of the Pan Am 103 bombing.

The bill sanctions foreign companies that provide new investments of over $40 million for the development of petroleum resources in Iran or Libya. The bill also sanctions foreign companies that violate existing U.N. prohibitions against trade with Libya in certain goods and services such as arms, oil equipment, and civil aviation services. If a violation occurs, the president is to impose two out of seven possible financial and trade sanctions against the violating company. Because of the extraterritoriality that is at the heart of ILSA, few U.S. allies support it, and some of their companies have found ways to circumvent it. In short, the United States has tried to quarantine Libya, but has been unsuccessful.

## The Story So Far...

Libya was not mentioned in the written scenario that simulation participants received ahead of time.

## At the Simulation

The Libyan plot line unfolded during the second half of the simulation. It introduced a classical foreign policy and security problem within a financial, economic, and international trade setting. The fictional script visualized some "Tom Clancy"–type events—and plenty of fog over what was actually going on. The Libyan channel had two dimensions. The first was specifically about an alleged Libyan nuclear weapons program. The Decision-Makers Group and the Foreign Policy and National Security Group received the following report: "Intelligence sources have revealed that Libya is developing a nuclear weapons capability based in large measure on imports of nuclear material from Russia brought in by the Russian Mafia." They also learned of unspecified contacts between Russian and Libyan scientists. However, the nature of the material received and the extent of knowledge of the Russian government in Moscow were unknown.

The second dimension of the plot line brought in economic, financial, and alliance complications. An indirect result of the financial turbulence and the spike in oil prices, this problem raised the specter of an initiative by the West European allies to broaden economic ties, or at least to turn a blind eye to domestic corporations trying to do more business with Libya. All simulation participants read this email:

> Upon learning that Libya may be developing nuclear weapons, Israeli lobbyists are actively engaging Congress to press for action against the threat of nuclear weapons in the entire region. At the same time, lobbyists for the airline industry are pressuring Congress to hold other countries accountable for violating the ILSA rules. Sources close to Boeing have reported that Daimler-Chrysler and Airbus have entered into several lucrative contracts with Libya that involve parts with dual-use technology.

Soon after, participants received a secret intelligence briefing via email that revealed that the European Union had agreed to a long-term purchase of Libyan energy resources that used a formula that would amount to a significant discount from world prices. Meanwhile, in public, a delegation of European trade officials stated that it would work to remove all economic sanctions on Libya.

These developments immediately touched off a blizzard of activity by simulation participants as they sought to determine what the appropriate U.S. policy response should be to each plot element. Sharp disagreements quickly became evident, both within and between the groups most directly involved in evaluating what policy options to adopt. Those deliberations were laced with a greater dispersion of viewpoints than on virtually any other policy problem considered over the course of the day.

## Tackling the Policy Problems

Within minutes of the report that the Russian mafia (or other rogue elements) had sold weapons-grade nuclear material to

Libya, the Foreign Policy and National Security Group pushed hard to gain more information, but those efforts became successively more muddled and frustrated since the information coming back from the Control Room was vague, incomplete, and often internally inconsistent. There was significant CIA experience in the simulation and a strong sense of what intelligence would probably be available if this sequence of developments had actually occurred in the real world. In the spirit of the simulation's mandate of presenting low-probability but high-cost events, however, the scenario envisaged an intelligence lapse that purposely would leave simulation participants in the dark about key elements.

What the Foreign Policy and National Security Group did then was to dispatch one of its most senior former diplomats to conduct a face-to-face interrogation of the Russian foreign minister, Igor Ivanov (once again, played by the Control Room). They pressed the minister: what did he know about a theft of Russian nuclear material and whether it had been sold to Libya? The Russian foreign minister had a prepared response. To paraphrase:

> Yes, it is true that there has been a theft of such material. Things are not entirely stable within Russia and while the overall crime rate is still far below that of the United States, thefts do happen. But the Russian government has no precise information on who perpetrated the theft and what they did with the stolen nuclear material. We have asked our friends in Libya and they assure us that they were not the recipient.

The emissary from the Foreign Policy and National Security Group then asked whether Russia would join the United States in a U.N. condemnation of Libya for a breech of the nuclear nonproliferation rules. The response was: "Not unless there is clear and convincing proof that Libya actually was the recipient, which Russia does not now have and probably won't be able to collect." Would Russia veto a U.S.-backed resolution condemning the purchaser? "We would have to consider it very carefully because we have no convincing information for us to doubt the word of our Libyan colleagues. Of course, if the United States found such information, we would not interfere with such a resolution." In short, the emissary was being stonewalled. When he returned to brief the Foreign Policy and National Security Group, the discussion took on a more bellicose tone.

After an animated internal discussion, the Foreign Policy and National Security Group followed up with a recommendation to the Decision-Makers Group that included four options: a full-scale blockade and embargo of Libyan oil shipments; preparations for an Israeli-type military action along the lines of the successful bombing attack on the French-built Osirik nuclear facility in 1981; a presidential order to move a carrier group out of Norfolk, Virginia, to the Mediterranean Sea; and as an intermediate step, presidential consultation with those European heads of government who had just announced the oil purchase agreement, in order to get their concurrence to share intelligence on the whereabouts of the stolen Russian nuclear material and to raise U.S. concerns about oil deals with the Libyans under these circumstances. They also recommended that the Immigration and Naturalization Service and the Customs Bureau be placed on high alert to guard against a potential terrorist attack on U.S. soil.

The Decision-Makers Group, with the secretary of defense taking the lead, agreed with the first and third options. Preparations for a general blockade or embargo were authorized, although they would not be implemented at this early stage. In addition, the recommended carrier battle group redeployment was ordered. But the Decision-Makers rejected consideration of an Osirik-like attack. For one thing, intelligence was too sketchy to permit accurate targeting. And the Decision-Makers were not inclined to press the Europeans on the oil purchase at a time when prices were still escalating.

The Foreign Policy and National Security Group was asked to prepare a public statement along the following lines. Until all the facts could be determined as to whether Libya was seeking to acquire nuclear materials, the United States said it "firmly opposes" the removal of economic sanctions on Libya and would use "all appropriate force" to enforce them "and such other steps as may be necessary." The Decision-Makers Group went on to request the State Department to inform privately the EU in Brussels as well as constituent governments that the United States would be moving forces to the Mediterranean to prepare for a general blockade of Libya, depending upon the outcome of the investigation of missing Russian nuclear weapons. They argued that the department should emphasize that if the EU were seen as thwarting steps the United States might have to take for our mutual security, it would produce an extraordinarily negative reaction in the executive branch and the Congress, as well as among the American people.

The Decision-Makers Group also asked for a special national intelligence estimate that would bring together all information available to the various U.S. intelligence agencies regarding the status of Libyan nuclear capabilities as well as any flow of additional technology to Libya, nuclear or otherwise. But the group's members concurred that, rather than wait for the result of that effort, a high-level delegation, including at least the deputy secretary of state, should go to Moscow and tell Russian President Vladimir Putin that one way or another he should see to it that the flow of nuclear material to Libya stops immediately and that he should punish those responsible. Otherwise, all U.S.-influenced aid to Russia, including IMF funding, would be halted immediately.

Meanwhile, members of the Decision-Makers Group felt that a report from "sources close to Boeing" was an insufficient basis on which to justify activating ILSA sanctions. The Economics and Trade Group had essentially come to the identical view as it considered the policy problem.

## The Control Room Perspective

The Libyan plot was intended to inject a classical foreign policy and security problem at a time when many simulation participants would be preoccupied by (and concentrating most of their energy and imagination on) the complex financial and economic issues at hand. That the discussions turned quickly to the consideration of military options testified to the practical experience of the people who participated in the simulation. After all, bombing nuclear facilities had been among the policy options considered in several real-life crisis spots in recent years, notably Iraq and North Korea. The decisions in those cases were to pursue diplomatic or economic options, and no bombs were dropped. Still, the August 1998 U.S. bombing of a pharmaceuticals factory in the Sudan on the basis of intelligence that it was producing chemical weapons was surely still fresh in the minds of simulation participants. Was that another instance of incomplete intelligence? Is it unrealistic to develop a scenario in which decisions have to be made without the luxury of full and complete information?

In an exercise grounded on the principle that conventional wisdom must always be challenged (even if in the end it is confirmed), it is always fair game for scenario writers to inject imperfect information, contradictions, and deception. The Decision-Makers Group chose a course of action—threatening Putin with a cut-off of aid if the flow of nuclear material was not stopped—that was warranted on the basis of minimal intelligence. The group was not going to wait until it could get on top of all the facts. As one simulation participant put it: "We decided to act as a superpower."

# Chapter X

# Plot Lines Involving China

## Real-World Backdrop

The 1990s was a period of perplexing contradictions in U.S.-China relations. Economic ties between the two countries galloped ahead. Spectacular growth in the volume of merchandise trade was most visible and often controversial, especially within the U.S. Congress. By the beginning of the new century, Chinese exports to the United States were exceeding $100 billion per year and the U.S. bilateral trade balance with China, at about $83 billion in deficit, was, for the first time in recent history, nearly parallel to the bilateral deficit of the United States with Japan.[1] But perhaps even more significant, and largely unforeseen at the beginning of the decade, was a tremendous expansion in direct investment in China by American corporations, rivaling that of other foreign corporations active in China for some time. U.S. firms injected some $30 billion into China over the decade.[2] They established manufacturing subsidiaries, entered into joint ventures with Chinese enterprises, and financed various types of what many corporate chief executives described as "strategic partnerships." Ironically, this increasingly fashionable business term seemed to have been appropriated by the Clinton administration to describe its evolving political relationship with China.

Even as economic and financial links broadened, there was a heightened awareness among business and financial people, as well as their professional advisers, of the deficiencies in the Chinese legal and regulatory infrastructure. There was also a recognition that, if disputes were to be avoided or resolved, it was desirable to incorporate the country more securely into the global system. The centerpiece of that effort was a determined effort to bring China into the World Trade Organization (WTO), which would subject China to an internationally agreed rule of law and insert a greater predictability into many aspects of the trade and investment relationship. To the surprise of many observers, the members within the Chinese hierarchy who were committed to modernizing China's economy agreed and took the lead in negotiating entry into the WTO, despite intense political opposition at home.

Alongside these positive trends, though, were a number of developments that injected considerable friction in the U.S.-China relationship. China was intent on carving out maritime sovereignty beyond internationally accepted norms. China was found to be selling weapons to countries that the United States had been designating as rogue states. A chronic source of tension was Taiwan. This came to a flash point in 1996, when China tested missiles near Taiwan and the United States responded by moving a substantial naval force into the area. While tensions subsided in the Taiwan Straits, the accidental bombing by NATO aircraft of the Chinese embassy in Belgrade during the Kosovo action in 1999 was harshly condemned by the Chinese government and unleashed a torrent of popular protest in China.

In short, the economic and financial pulses were offset, at least in part, by strains in the political and military realms. Further, the lack of transparency in the Chinese communist hierarchy made making predictions of future behavior extraordinarily difficult even for the most experienced experts in the U.S. government and the academic community.

Against this backdrop, China was featured in a number of plot lines in the simulation.

## Spratly Islands Incident

The members of the Decision-Makers Group and the Foreign Policy and National Security Group received a report saying that Chinese naval officers claimed that their vessels had been fired upon in the vicinity of the Spratly Islands. In the statement, the Chinese reserved the right to pursue and apprehend the perpetrators, even if it meant landing troops on one or more of the islands. Separately, members of the two groups also learned that U.S. intelligence sources had decoded a message from the Chinese foreign ministry to senior Japanese officials describing the Spratly incident in greater detail and hinting at a possible Chinese-Japanese joint venture to develop oil resources in the area. Simulation participants were asked what the United States response should be to the Chinese statements about the incident and to the report of Chinese overtures to Japan on codevelopment of oil fields in the area. The Foreign Policy and National Security Group's recommendation was to reiterate the current policy that stated that differences should be resolved by peaceful means and to discourage any use of troops by the Chinese.

## Devaluation of the Renminbi

Later in the game, simulation participants received by email the following digest of intelligence reports:

> Chinese leaders met in an emergency session to discuss the implications of the global financial crisis for China. They decided that the impact would be to worsen the internal financial sector disarray and probably touch off a global economic slowdown that would curb Chinese exports. They are agreed that the process of adapting the Chinese economy to the demands of WTO membership would also produce strains. And in the event that U.S. congressional opponents of normal trading relations between China and the United States prevailed, China would face additional difficulties—at least more restricted access to global capital markets. Therefore, it was decided to devalue the renminbi by 35 percent.

Participants were asked whether the United States should condemn, support, or be neutral toward the Chinese devaluation.

Simulation participants recognized that such a large devaluation of the Chinese currency would put significant competitive pressure on the debt-troubled Asian countries that were already in far worse financial shape than China. The participants recommended that the United States be proactive and emphasize to the Chinese authorities that further devaluation would be unhelpful. They felt that the communication should clearly state their view that economic stability in the region is important to both nations and that a perspective broader than the narrow question of Chinese export prospects should be considered. However, they also wanted to reassure the Chinese that their views and concerns were of great importance to the international community and that the United States was prepared to take action to make it possible for Chinese leaders to attend the upcoming Economic Summit of the major industrial countries. The original seven-country gathering, including the United States, the United Kingdom, Canada, France, Germany, and Italy, had already incorporated Russian participation in the mid-1990s, and an inclusion of China would signify a maturation of Chinese economic and financial involvement in the global system.

Shortly after making this recommendation, simulation participants were briefed about the strong adverse reaction the Chinese devaluation had provoked throughout Asia, the United States, and elsewhere. Several members of the U.S. House of Representatives had issued a statement that the Chinese devaluation was a "hostile, 'beggar-thy-neighbor' policy act." China already had a very large trade surplus with the United States, nearly $100 billion per year. The devaluation would only serve to worsen this imbalance. As a result, a number of members of Congress were in favor of restricting Chinese imports until the Chinese financial authorities reversed their policy. Participants were pressed on whether the U.S. government should publicly repudiate or express approval for such an approach.

After some deliberation, participants decided that the president should dissuade Congress from such a course of action. Instead, they proposed that he buttress private representations to individual members of Congress with a public statement arguing that the current turmoil in the financial markets made it an inopportune time to start a trade war. In the meantime, simulation participants dictated that the White House should follow up with a private communication to the Chinese authorities encouraging them to accelerate the economic reforms necessary to be admitted to the WTO. They reasoned that such an action would be a positive step and would help defuse any congressional efforts to impose trade restrictions.

## Taiwan Independence Debate

The Decision-Makers Group and the Foreign Policy and National Security Group received the following email briefing: "Intelligence sources have learned that the new Taiwanese administration has decided that the time is appropriate to declare independence from China. They have made the calculation that, in the general atmosphere of questioning U.S. global leadership and authority following the financial convulsions of recent months, the United States would have no choice but to stand by Taiwan, regardless of the PRC reaction." The simulation participants were asked to consider how the United States should respond to the Taiwanese decision.

The Foreign Policy and National Security Group discussed three options: do not come to the defense of the Taiwanese because U.S. public opinion will not tolerate the casualties that would inevitably follow the military confrontation that would likely ensue; assert that the United States should publicly support a democratically elected government and a long-standing ally, because otherwise promises of U.S. defense would be meaningless with the rest of its allies; and allow the Taiwanese to declare independence if they desire, but tell them that at any moment we could cut them off from further trade and military assistance and publicly embrace the Chinese position, so as to improve our relationship with China.

After weighing these three options, the Foreign Policy and National Security Group recommended sending a senior envoy to Taiwan with instructions to inform the Taiwanese that the United States would not help defend them if they declared independence unilaterally. The Decision-Makers Group concurred: "Tell the Taiwanese to cool it."

# Notes

1. U.S. Census Bureau, FTD: U.S. Trade Balance with China; U.S. Trade Balance with Japan.

2. Bureau of Economic Analysis, *Survey of Current Business* (September 2000), Table 16—U.S. Direct Investment Abroad, 87.

# Chapter XI

# Other Plot Lines: Financial Institutions in Difficulty

The preceding chapters have gone through what the organizers and simulation participants considered to be the main policy problems that cut across financial, economic, foreign policy, and security lines. There were many other plot lines that were important in their own terms and did generate active debate within the various groups. But for various reasons they were dealt with expeditiously, or were viewed as less compelling analytically or lacking implications for the functioning of the global financial and economic system as a whole. This chapter summarizes what those problems were and briefly notes how they were resolved.

We purposely did not include a case in which a traditional regulated U.S. financial institution—a commercial bank, a savings and loan, or a securities firm—was the focal point of the problem. Among the talented, experienced professionals in the Financial Regulatory Group and the Central Banking Group were individuals who had been through such failures in the past, often numerous times, and they would have known what to do to deal with troubled banks or brokerage houses. Instead, we tried to pose problems mainly through the lens of financial institutions that were *not* conventional, regulated entities. Also we put the emphasis on American institutions that were primarily foreign owned and controlled, in order to raise the issue of whose regulatory authority would give them principal responsibility for dealing with the problem. We left open the possibility that there was no primary regulator at all, either at the parent or the affiliate level.

In all, there were four additional plot lines involving financial institutions in difficulty that were not covered in the country chapters:

1. A British insurance company's U.S. affiliate specializing in buying and selling financial derivatives (futures, forwards, swaps, options, and complex securities based on one or more of them) that got into difficulty.

2. An Asian financial conglomerate with a profitable U.S. finance company subsidiary that was engaged in taking capital out of the U.S. affiliate in order to offset losses it had incurred.

3. A German government-initiated facility to provide guarantees to creditors of troubled Berlin real estate projects.

4. A sizable Malaysian bank whose owners' shares were seized by the Malaysian government.

Here is how the groups dealt with them:

## Troubled U.S. Financial Derivatives Specialist with a Parent British Insurance Company

The financial regulators and central bankers learned that the U.S. securities affiliate of a major British insurance firm announced it was temporarily withdrawing from the business of making a market in equity derivatives for hedge funds and other high-octane portfolio managers. The news had prompted a scramble on the part of leveraged equity investors and participants in equity derivatives to replace maturing contracts that could not be rolled over with either the American affiliate or its British parent. Among the counterparties in derivative transactions were several small and medium-size U.S. regional banks that had substantial profit positions with respect to the affiliate. They had told members of Congress that they feared being left out of a settlement and were unprepared to risk a bankruptcy court's adjudication of their claims. A further large counterparty was a U.S. defense contractor with substantial unhedged options outstanding. The groups were asked what kind of support the U.S. government should be prepared to supply, or help arrange, in order to limit the adverse consequences.

In response, the groups bombarded the Control Room with questions:

*Question* from the financial regulators: Would the parent stand behind the U.S. affiliate?

*Answer*: The parent does not know the full extent of exposure of the subsidiary because of the inherent complexity of contingent options.*

*Question* from both the financial regulators and the central bankers: We would like to know the severity of the British insurance company's difficulties and the degree of derivatives exposure of its U.S. affiliate.

*Answer*: The insurance company has total assets of 260 billion pounds and total equity of 32 billion pounds. The derivatives book of the U.S. subsidiary is U.S. $500 billion. Estimates of the potential loss to counterparties from nonperformance is a maximum of U.S. $75 billion. These figures represent the outer limit of losses to counterparties at current market values if none of the outstanding contracts is performed. The management of the subsidiary believes that the actual losses would be considerably less with official support because it will be able to work out contracts over the next six months, limiting losses substantially.

---

* Contingent options are not simple puts or calls, but have a complex structure of payoffs that depends on whether other specified events take place.

*Question*: What are the U.K. regulatory authorities, the Financial Services Authority (FSA), and the Bank of England doing about this?

*Answer*: The FSA believes that financial support by both the Bank of England and the U.S. authorities will be necessary to avert large-scale abrogation of existing contracts. The Bank of England believes the problems of the U.S. subsidiary with its financial derivatives business must be dealt with by the insurer and the local U.S. regulators.

The Central Banking Group made the following public statement: "We are in contact with the FSA and the Bank of England about the appropriate action to be taken with respect to this situation. We will make decisions as we learn more. We stand ready to provide liquidity if it should be necessary." The financial regulators took a tough line when they announced: "We will take steps to enforce the responsibility of the U.K. parent for the financial condition of its U.S. affiliates and their outstanding positions in the marketplace."

Clearly, the ultimate resolution of the problem depends on the actions and realistic alternatives of many players not part of the game: the British insurer may be too financially crippled to aid the U.S. affiliate even if it wanted to; the Bank of England may not be in a position to provide even temporary financing without the approval of the U.K. Chancellor of the Exchequer; and some counterparties may not be able to wait and may be forced to go to court in the United States to protect their interests. But from the point of view of the U.S. financial authorities, they have signified their intentions and have put a road map in place to which others could refer. Could the incident have systemic implications? From what was learned at the simulation, it was unlikely but still could not be dismissed out of hand.

## Asian Conglomerate Seeks to Decapitalize U.S. Affiliate

The Financial Regulators Group learned of reports that a troubled Asian financial conglomerate held a controlling interest in a profitable finance company in the United States and had instructed the U.S. affiliate to remit a sizable portion of its capital to the holding company parent. This withdrawal of capital would drastically impair the financial position of this U.S. affiliate. The U.S. unit had substantial credit relationships with major U.S. banks and securities firms. Were there any grounds, they were asked, to block the transfer or to approve it only under specified conditions?

After probing the situation further, the financial regulators were able to piece together some additional information. The Asian conglomerate had its holding company headquartered in Taiwan. It owned an insurance company, two offshore banks in Jersey and the Cayman Islands, and a proprietary trading operation that had many features of a hedge fund. The conglomerate itself was unregulated. However, there were significant loans from major U.S. banks to the outfit, and its commercial paper was widely held in retail mutual funds. If the holding company parent were to be downgraded by the credit ratings agencies, those mutual funds would not be able to hold the paper going forward. But even before they could complete their investigation, the publicly traded debt of the Asian financial conglomerate was downgraded from A to B minus.

Additional reports were soon making the rounds to the decision-makers and to the financial regulators. It was learned that important contributors to both political parties in the United States had made known that they stood to lose substantial sums of money if the problems of the Asian financial conglomerate were not handled successfully. They had warned that they were appealing to friends in Congress and the administration to take an active interest in this unfolding financial mishap. At about the same time, intelligence sources reported that the institution was involved in money laundering and the transference of funds for possibly illegal political donations. The financial regulators were asked for their expert advice on two issues: What might be the liability of the U.S. finance company should the money laundering charges turn out to be valid? And should the U.S.

government encourage the parent to sell the profitable U.S. finance company outright rather than decapitalize it?

The financial regulators advised the "White House" that the U.S. government should not directly try to force the holding company to sell, but that they would suggest contacting major creditors in the United States to cooperate in encouraging the holding company to sell the American affiliate. As for the money laundering charge, they concluded that there would be no legal liability unless the finance company was directly involved. And even if they did have knowledge of what was going on, it would be a matter for the Justice Department, not the financial regulatory agencies.

Finally, no one volunteered to take up the matter of campaign contributions, at least at this stage.

## German Government-Initiated Real Estate Credit Facility

The central bankers and financial regulators were briefed that the German government, in collaboration with the major German banking institutions and real estate investors, had established a new entity for providing guarantees to creditors of troubled Berlin real estate projects. Overbuilding of offices and commercial buildings in Berlin in anticipation of the transfer of the German federal government agencies from Bonn had reached alarming proportions. The new facility would provide for profit sharing for the German public authorities in the event of a rebound of real estate values. The facility would not, however, be open to financial institutions headquartered outside the European Union and Switzerland. Thus, U.S. and other foreign creditors, if they had lent to or invested in the real estate sector, would be expected to make their own arrangements with the real estate developers, who are at risk of defaulting on their obligations. They also learned that the European Central Bank was cooperating with the German workout arrangement because of the European-wide appeal. There was little or nothing the Central

Banking Group could do about the program. The financial regulators sought to commence discussions with the German securities regulatory group but otherwise could find no technical reason to oppose the arrangement. It would be a political decision whether or not to register disapproval, not a technical matter.

## Malaysia Seizes Partnership Shares of Private Malaysian Bank

The Decision-Makers Group and the Economics and Trade Group were told that a well-known and highly respected American businessman—and partner of a Malaysian entrepreneur operating mainly out of Singapore—has told his administration friends that the Mahathir government has taken over without compensation the partnership's shares in a sizable Malaysian bank. The ownership rights have been voided by decree. The American businessman asked whether the U.S. government could use its influence to reverse this breach of due process and to restore the property rights of the partnership.

The Economics and Trade Group members were divided, but most of the group felt that the U.S. government should not intervene in this crisis. The bank seizure did not have significant global economic implications, and the group felt that the businessman in question should seek redress through the local courts or through standard embassy channels. A dissenting viewpoint maintained that some emerging market governments might be tempted to take similar actions in their own countries unless a clear public example was made in the Malaysian case. Both sides agreed that the administration should show concern and make a public statement about the general importance of protecting property rights. But the recommendation to the decision-makers was that the United States should not intervene any further.

# Chapter XII

# Lessons and Implications for Policymaking

### Reviewing the Real-World Context

It is useful to recall how the "game" was played and to become reacquainted with the real-life geopolitical and geoeconomic backdrop against which our fictional, future-oriented scenario was superimposed. It is a world in which the issues, the values, and the very vocabulary of economics and markets have gradually displaced the life-and-death absolutes of the Cold War and their hold over the making of foreign policy and national security decisions.

In reality, the extent of this paradigm shift is more sweeping, though also subtler, than many observers of the post–Cold War global system have appreciated. It is not merely a matter of lifting economics to a more influential position in defining our national interests and priorities. After all, that trend was firmly in place long ago, perhaps most strikingly during the successive oil shocks of the 1970s that put the U.S. economy, and indeed all advanced economies, heavily at risk.

What is distinctive in the first post–Cold War decade is the increasing centrality of the role of modern financial markets in the evolution of national economies and in the development of an international economy. For the first thirty years after World War II, various steps were taken to open up the international trading system, through such highly successful multilateral endeavors as the Kennedy Round and the Tokyo Round of trade liberalization. But well into the 1970s, the rules of the international monetary system, as enshrined in the IMF Articles of Agreement, legitimized the use of a wide range of restrictions on the flows of capital. Foreign exchange controls were common even among most major industrial countries until the early 1980s. Most capital flows to the developing countries came from official sources, such as the World Bank or official export credit agencies such as the U.S. Export-Import Bank. Only after the oil price shocks of the 1970s did large-scale loans by internationally active commercial banks begin to be made, loans funded by the recycling of what were commonly known as "petrodollars."

By the end of the Cold War era, conditions were entirely transformed. Financial capital was free to move around the globe with minimal barriers. The very structure of world financial markets underwent fundamental change, and their role in allocating capital dramatically increased. The magnitude of money capable of coursing through the global markets; the speed with which money can move; the increasing number of countries and companies with at least some access to this global credit creation engine; the awesome mathematics and computer technology that is enlisted in facilitating a tremendous volume of transactions; the widespread media coverage and public awareness of current events; and the relative weakness of official supervisory and regulatory mechanisms for overseeing all of this—these developments were all unprecedented.

Today, modern financial markets are armed with a double-edged sword. They are a force for considerable good—by mobilizing financial capital and expertise they have the ability to facilitate economic transformation and growth. But they carry a powerful and exasperating downside—unstable market expectations characterized by enhanced volatility when market perceptions abruptly change. Repeated crises of varying degrees of severity reverberated through Mexico in 1994–95, all of Asia in 1997–98, then Russia and Brazil in 1998, and just recently Argentina and Turkey. In every case, what began as financial traumas soon broadened out to infect the economies of these countries and, almost always, their political systems as well. Political leadership has turned over—in Mexico's case for the first time in seventy years—in nearly every country that was a victim of global financial turbulence.

Even in the United States, a country that was largely spared financial trauma in the past ten years until the recent travails of the high-tech sector of the stock market in 2000–01, a growing number of people are uneasy about the economic and financial outlook. Many now agree with the proposition that our way of life can be threatened more by a severe, sustained fall in the value of our financial assets than by the aggression of some future, unspecified enemy. And even considering the favorable legacy of economic prosperity and financial gains during the Clinton years, a new administration must be alert to the widespread effect a market downturn might have.

The record of the 1990s has verified one intuitive proposition: when financial markets are functioning well, when the confidence of investors is high, and when capital is liberally supplied, economic growth is exemplary. That is true in the case of capital flows to emerging markets such as Latin America, Asia, and Africa or to transitional economies like those of Russia, Poland, or the Czech Republic, or even to the United States itself. Conversely, a sudden loss of confidence, suspension of capital inflows, and repatriation of foreign investments is enormously difficult to handle; under such circumstances, there are no routine or painless policy remedies.

What is not resolved is how governments of the various countries will react to such perturbations in market sentiment and to the associated swings in the flows of private capital. Do they become more receptive to the case for opening up their markets when times are good, or only under the unremitting pressure of financial distress? Do our relations with debt-troubled countries improve when we overlook their policy shortcomings and provide generous emergency funding, or rather when we hold fast to our principles and insist on needed reforms that will have long-term positive effects? Based on the past decade of experience, there is evidence to support both sides.

Our exploration of financial vulnerabilities and their interconnections with broader economic, foreign policy, and national security considerations assumes that the ascendancy of economics and markets, if not irreversible, will not be reversed any time soon. Economics and market forces will play an increasing role in the setting of foreign policy objectives, priorities, strategies, and responses to the inevitable crises that lie ahead.

These forces will also have a decisive role in reshaping our relations with traditional allies. Our allies will naturally be going through a similar exercise themselves. Without an obvious common enemy demanding unified opposition, it is likely that the goals, priorities, and interests of our allies will increasingly differ from ours. Over time, this divergence of interests will lead to disagreements, misunderstandings, and occasional policy incoherence, even outright rupture on certain issues. It already happens from time to time in the arena of trade, and it requires a formal dispute resolution system, the WTO, to prevent individual cases from poisoning otherwise mutually beneficial trade relations. It is bound to happen in the financial arena with increasing frequency in the future and with unforeseeable consequences for our overall foreign relations.

The question for policymakers is how to get better prepared for this new generally peaceful, but irregularly fractious world. It is a world in which economic and financial instability, by itself or through its impact on political stability abroad, poses a major threat to the broadly defined security of the United States. Better preparedness requires policymakers, and the economic and financial experts who advise them, to become more knowledgeable about the political context in which foreign governments must operate. It is especially important to understand the constraints limiting the ability of these governments to act forcefully and with foresight during periods of intense economic and financial distress. Better preparedness equally requires foreign policy experts to develop genuine expertise about economics and markets, by gaining a sophisticated understanding of how they function in normal times and how they malfunction during times of strain.

Our goal in organizing the simulation was to create a method for preparing policymakers to be able to better identify the vulnerabilities within the global system that make individual countries or entire regions susceptible to shocks. This required an entirely new way of thinking about potential stress points. As Council on Foreign Relations President Les Gelb said: "Policymakers have got to play economic and financial war games with the same intensity that they used to play old war games in the national security field." Done well, the payoff to this kind of crosscutting effort will be in minimizing the probability of future crises or, failing that, in lessening the adverse consequences when they do erupt.

Such an interdisciplinary approach has notable precedents. It would loosely parallel the innovations in foreign policy and national security thinking that emerged at the height of the Cold War. By the late 1950s, traditional diplomatic skills were seen as inadequate for the task of responding to challenges posed by a determined, nuclear-armed, ideological adversary, the Soviet Union. In response, a new intellectual foundation for considering the interface between military planning, geopolitical analysis, science and technology, and defense economics was needed to consider what could be done to improve U.S. national security in the face of the relentless Soviet threat. This laid the foundation for a principled case for arms control and the adoption of a strategy to achieve it. Beyond that, responsibility for these kinds of crosscutting issues was institutionalized by the expanded role and influence of the National Security Council and its head, the national security adviser. Along the same general lines, just recently, the increasing interrelationship between economics and foreign policy was formally recognized by the Bush administration in its formation of a new post to coordinate and integrate international economic policy with national security and foreign policy: the deputy assistant to the president for international economic affairs and deputy national security adviser.*

Our exercise was also inspired by new risk-management techniques adopted by forward-thinking corporations and financial institutions in the United States and abroad. These businesses undergo extensive exercises intended to stress test their operating systems, their market positions relative to competitors, their portfolios of businesses, and their financial assets and liabilities. Going beyond statistical modeling, which inevitably tells companies more about the past events than future possibilities, risk analysts in the corporate world have chosen to construct scenarios that challenge their own assumptions and make it possible to focus on improbable, but potentially highly costly, events. Policymakers in government can benefit from the same process.

## Observations from the Simulation

The seventy-five individuals who spent an entire Saturday in January 2000 at the Council on Foreign Relations working together to solve complex domestic economic and foreign policy problems not only taught us much about the way to handle crises, but they also affirmed the value of simulations in the policy realm. Armed only with the knowledge that was put forth in the fictional scenario, "The Story So Far . . .," players worked through the consequences of a major financial disturbance, confronted current events that often challenged U.S. interests, and collaborated within and among their groups to formulate U.S. foreign policy.

---

* President Bush's appointee to this post, Gary R. Edson, serves as a deputy to both Lawrence Lindsey, the assistant to the president for economic policy, and Condoleezza Rice, the assistant to the president for national security affairs. The position, according to Bush aides, will "make it easier for the president to recognize and respond to potentially destabilizing financial crises like those that occurred in Mexico, Asia, and Russia." "Bush Creating New White House Post," The Associated Press, Wednesday, January 17, 2001; http://quest.cjonline.com/stories/011701/gen_0117017759.shtml.

What generalizations are warranted about the way players approached the game and dealt with the policy dilemmas thrust at them? From discussions with participants and colleagues and from listening to tape-recorded interchanges from the simulation, six conclusions stand out:

1.  The overarching priority of simulation participants was to deal with the financial crisis, even if it meant subordinating issues that might, in other circumstances, have justified undivided attention. Without first restoring stability in the markets and reducing the potential for subsequent negative economic consequences, there was a clear sense that policies to address other problems would be less effective. Some participants argued, with considerable justification, that the time pressure of the simulation was responsible for channeling the policy discussion so narrowly toward the financial crisis, but others believed it reflected an honest assessment of priorities.

2.  The participants took on the mantle of the United States as the lone superpower comfortably and without being told to do so. The practical significance was that on most issues there was a predilection to get involved, to try to help to resolve the problems of other countries, and to recommend solutions regardless of whether they were specifically solicited. It follows that there were very few people who thought to leave certain problems alone to allow them to run their course without intervention. In the hurry-up atmosphere of a simulation, with problems flaring up rapidly in one part of the world after another, the tendency of most participants was to *do* something.

3.  Desire for involvement did not always translate into assertive policy execution. To be sure, sometimes decisions were made with supreme self-confidence, as in the cases of the response to Saudi Arabian foreign policy initiatives, to Turkish threats to limit future U.S. military use of the

Incrlik Air Base, or to the alleged Libyan importation of stolen Russian nuclear materials. But in other cases, as Marc Levinson, the simulation's National Security Council staff director, noted, "this firmness was not so apparent." He cited the Turkish financial situation, the Brazilian debt moratorium, and the collapse of the Asian financial conglomerate with vague ties to U.S. political figures as examples in which an arrogant superpower might have been more inclined to shape events to its own liking. According to Levinson's personal observations on the results of the simulation: "This indicates a basic institutional bias: if you're a superpower, geopolitical problems are easy to solve, economic problems are not, so you should focus on geopolitical problems. . . . It is difficult for the government (certainly at the decision-maker level) to act as a hegemon part of the time and as a member of a collaborative group the rest of the time."

4. Participants were generally reluctant to step back from the rush of events and policy problems and to try putting developments into a broad intellectual context—a fault of many real-world policymakers. However, there was at least one conspicuous exception during the simulation. At one point, the Foreign Policy and National Security Group was blessed with a lull in the tempo of new problems and devoted considerable effort to thinking outside the box. Group members decided it would be worthwhile to assess the problems that were unfolding more broadly and to consider the international relevance of the events taken as a whole. They went so far as to draft a memo to the president discussing these global opportunities and risks. However, as is often the case in the real world of Washington bureaucracy, their work did not get anywhere. Their counterparts in the Decision-Makers Group were too tied up with the details of crisis response to process the memo.

5.  What particularly concerned the decision-makers were those plot lines in which the United States was discriminated against or otherwise treated unfairly.

The written scenario rested on the unstated premise that allies and adversaries alike had bottled-up resentments that they could not express as long as the U.S. economy was robust and financial markets were strong. But these resentments manifested themselves in various ways once the United States showed signs of vulnerability. The hypothesized financial crises created difficulties for all nations, but especially for the United States. The puncturing of American hubris provided a setting that permitted some of these resentments to surface.

Several events in the plot were inserted explicitly in order to find out what would happen if the United States was eager to negotiate with other countries but was ignored. For instance, anticipating that the Central Banking Group would seek to negotiate a common interest rate strategy with its foreign counterparts, we set it up so that the European Central Bank would decline to negotiate. The Europeans insisted that interest rate cuts could only occur on the condition of a substantial rebound in the value of their common currency, the euro. Late in the simulation the euro did rally, and the Central Banking Group was informed that the ECB had followed through exactly as promised. The ECB acted unilaterally, however, not as part of a coordinated action.

A second manifestation of this theme was in the pivotal Brazilian plot line. In the scenario, participants read that Brazil was faced with heavy new capital outflows as contagion spread worldwide. After the simulation began, they received reports that Brazilian financial authorities had decided that their official foreign currency reserves were insufficient to service all their existing external debt and that the authorities had sought a voluntary debt rescheduling agreement with bond holders. European and Asian creditors came to terms. U.S. creditors held out for more favorable treatment. Brazil decided to up the ante by refusing to pay them anything.

When the decision-makers learned of the breakdown in relations between Brazil and the U.S. bondholders, they quickly recognized the potential for discriminatory treatment based on the nationality of the bondholder and recognized that it could set a dangerous example and draw imitators. Plus, there was a palpable and very human reaction to foreign discrimination against Americans. Participants found the unequal treatment intolerable, even though they clearly sympathized with the plight of the Brazilians at a time of global financial turbulence. Some of the decision-makers were willing to go so far as to threaten economic sanctions against Brazil in order to force them to reverse the policy.

There is an important lesson in the resolution of this story. The American anger at being discriminated against was meliorated by the Brazilians' willingness to negotiate—and by their modest request that the U.S. government play a mediating role in urging U.S. creditors to return to the bargaining table. When, later in the simulation, top Wall Street financiers approached the Treasury to reveal that they too wanted to negotiate an end to the impasse with Brazil, the Treasury secretary readily agreed to help restart discussions.

6.  The main conclusion that came out of the simulation is that even an extraordinarily complicated chain of events, with substantial and widespread adverse consequences, can be managed intelligently using familiar policy instruments. And participants in the simulation were confident in their decisions. Even in retrospect, most were satisfied that they had not overlooked superior courses of action even in the turmoil of rapidly moving events.

My personal judgment is that the success of the simulation reinforces one of the lessons that I draw from the repeated financial crises in the second half of the 1990s—namely, that crisis management is systematically more tractable than crisis prevention. Crisis prevention is the harder task for many reasons, but primarily because of the sheer magnitude of the information one needs to collect and interpret in order to assess a complex and changing situation. It is far easier to get the IMF to write a big check than it is to put in place the institutional mechanisms to prevent domestic banks from excessive lending, to discourage domestic corporations from over-leveraging their balance sheets, or to keep the government from distorting budgetary practices in order to indirectly subsidize favored corporate interests. But the rewards for successfully identifying financial vulnerabilities and taking early action to contain and control them are potentially enormous. Those rewards, in the economic and financial realm, can be measured in terms of preserving jobs, maintaining satisfactory rates of economic growth, and improving living standards. And in the foreign policy and security arena they can be measured in terms of reduced international friction and a lessened threat of hostilities.

## How Best to Organize a Scenario-Based Simulation

We learned a lot about the mechanics of conducting an elaborate international financial war game. Naturally, the most important ingredients for a successful policy simulation are an imaginative scenario full of challenging policy problems, and experienced, congenial individuals willing to take the whole exercise seriously. Plus, in order to have an email based system for information dissemination and for facilitating communications among the organizers and the various groups of participants, you need a sophisticated computerized information network staffed by talented people.

Beyond those general points, I would put special emphasis on the construction of the scenario. The trick is to confront conventional wisdom with challenging, unlikely, and imaginary events. This is no easy task.

Months in advance we convened a number of Council on Foreign Relations experts to help us come up with a scenario that would fit these criteria.

Our starting point was to identify the conventional wisdom of the day—essentially, the market and political setting as of the end of 1999. The sentiment was one of optimism, if not infallibility; the financial and economic debris of the Asian debacle had been cleaned up, Brazil was getting back in shape, and even Russia appeared to be coming out of its self-inflicted financial convulsion. Few thought that the United States—with its strong economy, low and falling unemployment, modest inflation, firm dollar, stable political configuration, impressive government budgetary surplus, credible monetary policy, and awe-inspiring stock market—could be significantly harmed by international financial turmoil.*

In addition to verbalizing the conventional wisdom, we felt it important to identify vulnerabilities in the U.S. financial markets, if there were any at all. For that purpose, we held a round-table discussion with market experts and scholars in September 1999 and a follow-up session in November 1999. Beyond calling attention to the large and growing U.S. trade and current-account deficit and the recent increase in private-sector debt, the general message was that the United States had things under pretty good control. Household and corporate net worth had ballooned faster than debt burdens. Banks and other major financial institutions were well capitalized, profitable, and becoming increasingly better equipped to manage credit risk through their use of computer-modeled stress tests. (That was well before anyone asked about leverage in the telecoms or electric power sectors.) In the winter of 2000, even the meeting convened to address vulnerabilities in the U.S. markets adjourned with a tone of confidence.

---

* In the fall of 1999, the handful of contrarians who suggested that there was a bubble in the stock market, or at least its high-tech wing, were widely scorned either as self-promoters, fuddy-duddies, or reactionary. But market sentiment changes quickly. By the beginning of 2000, the notion that stock prices were unsustainably high was not so easily dismissed. The attrition in equity values over the subsequent fifteen months, especially in high-flying Nasdaq tech stocks, was a chastening experience for numerous investors and pundits alike.

Early in the drafting of the scenario, we decided to inject plot elements that would test many aspects of the highly optimistic, and demonstrably complacent, conventional view. We identified major areas of growth and focused on creating problems that would specifically test those sectors. For this reason, we generated a slowdown in the seemingly untouchable high-tech capital expenditures. The scenario envisioned computer orders suddenly slipping away following the Y2K protection effort; positive inflation performance threatened by a rise in labor and energy costs; and the firm dollar undermined by outflows of foreign capital that had long been invested in U.S. securities. There was also a reemergence of inflationary concerns that precipitated a sell-off in the U.S. bond market, where numerous foreign investors held huge stakes and were sensitive to risk. Finally, the stock market was stung first by the presumed downturn in the high-tech sector and then by the start of substantial selling by domestic and foreign investors caught off guard by such rapid change in both fundamentals and market psychology.

Those skeptical about the value of scenarios as a business or government policy planning tool properly point out that it is impossible to know in advance precisely how a crisis—financial, economic or political—will unfold. That caveat is valid, but only up to a point. Perfect foresight is unnecessary. In order to motivate a productive simulation exercise, it is only required that the scenario be plausible and challenging, not that it be prescient. If it turns out later that certain plot elements in the scenario actually occur in the real world, as was the case for some aspects of our scenario, so much the better. But as a practical matter, it is sufficient that simulation participants believe the story line is worth pursuing. Ours met that test.

Regrettably, a credible scenario also has to leave out a lot of the more creative plot elements. Our associates at the Council volunteered a large number of fascinating, highly imaginative plot twists that were not included because they seemed at the time either to be too fanciful or too compelling. We feared that simulation participants would have either ridiculed them or dropped everything else to dig into them. Accordingly, we ruled out highly dramatic developments such as assassination attempts or a failure of one of the world's biggest banks. We also were careful to avoid plot lines that inadvertently might have stumbled onto potentially delicate real-world concerns. For example, we were urged to consider a plot line centered around the Osama bin Laden organization, the sources of its funding, and fictional intelligence reports of plans for future terrorist assaults on U.S. facilities. We decided against that on the grounds that government agencies likely were already considering contingencies involving bin Laden and others linked to his group.

Now, a year later, it is possible to see that some of the events we imagined in our fictional scenario have actually occurred in the real world. Turkey has had a severe banking crisis, and its December 1998 IMF program has had to go through wholesale revision. Argentina has had exactly the kind of capital flight feared by its fictitious officials during the game. The result has been a new, massive financing package to Argentina from the IMF and other public-sector and private-sector financial institutions. Ukraine has fallen farther into arrears on required payments to Russia for natural gas, further straining relations between the two former Soviet republics. There has even been a hung presidential election. However, in this case, the scenario got it wrong. The hung election was not in Mexico, as posited in the fictional scenario, but in the United States!

# Appendix A

# The Story So Far ...

## Hypothetical Scenario for January 22, 2000, Policy Simulation

In the months prior to April 2000, when financial markets were jolted by a rush of events that touched off severe turbulence, there had been considerable talk in the papers and in financial circles that the risks were mounting of an unsustainable bubble in the U.S. stock market. Sophisticated investors had begun to consider more seriously that they should be more actively diversifying the currency composition of their global financial assets in order to hedge their bets against a possible setback in the U.S. markets. At about the same time, there was a growing feeling in the foreign policy community around the world that the United States, with unbridled self-confidence because of the strong economy and a persistent advance in financial wealth, was embracing an unwelcome form of unilateralism in its relations with other countries. This was producing an undercurrent of resentment and predisposed a number of countries, including long-time American allies, to contemplate courses of action to counter what was often referred to as "American triumphalism." This is the general setting for the financial and economic developments that would soon create complex policy problems—not only for the official institutions that normally deal with financial and economic matters, but also for the areas of government responsible for U.S. foreign policy and national security.

The financial turmoil started in the United States with repeated rounds of heavy selling of equities and fixed-income securities. However, it quickly spread to envelop practically every major financial center and market. Hardly any type of investment vehicle was spared.

Among the triggering factors were news of a rise in U.S. inflation, prompting market concern of a tightening of American monetary policy and reports of a sell-off of mutual funds as individuals sought to raise cash to pay higher-than-expected income taxes. Also frequently mentioned by commentators were the announcements by leading PC manufacturers and software providers of a large, unexpected plunge in new orders for their products. Feared problems associated with the Y2K conversion had not materialized. In reassessing their technology needs, business managers from the largest to the smallest enterprises concluded that they had built up sufficient capacity for their operations and could lower new acquisitions by an average of 30 percent. They intended to maintain support for business applications utilizing the Internet. But market optimism about future rapid growth in e-commerce was shaken by a spate of technical glitches that effectively blocked most transactions over the Internet during a sixteen-hour period in late March.

Unlike some previous episodes when share prices of high-tech companies started to slip, on this occasion their slide pulled down the broader market indexes. The *Wall Street Journal* published a report asserting that some attorneys had approached regulators in Washington to forewarn them that class action suits were being prepared against a number of the largest private pension funds in the United States for breaching fiduciary duties. The suits would allege that the corporate executives responsible for directing the investment of the pension fund assets had disregarded investment guidelines set by their respective boards of directors. Instead, they had allowed the proportion of equities in their funds' portfolios to rise well above the prescribed limits, essentially by failing to rebalance equity to asset ratios over the period when the stock market was rallying. The news prompted numerous pension fund overseers to take immediate steps to get within their own board guidelines, accentuating the sell-off in the marketplace.

Meanwhile, managers of a U.S. securities affiliate of a major British insurance company with global portfolio holdings that had been active making a market in equity derivatives for hedge funds and other high-octane portfolios announced that the affiliate was temporarily withdrawing from that business pending a thorough review of its exposures. The news prompted a scramble on the part of leveraged equity investors and participants in equity derivatives to replace maturing contracts that could not be rolled over either with the American affiliate or with its British parent.

That parent insurance company also revealed that it had been selling long Treasuries, bunds, and gilts to raise liquidity. This touched off a surge of activity in the bond market. The fixed-income markets in the United States, Europe, and Japan were further unsettled by reports that OPEC ministers, meeting in Vienna, had agreed on production cutbacks sufficient to maintain oil prices above the $30 a barrel level. As a result, the yield on thirty-year U.S. Treasury obligations was driven up to its highest levels since 1994.

With uncertainties multiplying, the Federal Reserve issued a statement that it stood ready to inject whatever liquidity was required to protect the safety and soundness of the system, notwithstanding the recent lift in the rate of consumer price inflation to above 4 percent per year. However, the European Central Bank (ECB) ended its scheduled policy meeting without a public expression of support for the Fed's action. Two members of the ECB privately told journalists that they were concerned about the potential moral hazard engendered by an "asymmetric" policy toward asset prices, as seemed to be practiced by the U.S. central bank.

Concerned that the Federal Reserve was abandoning an anti-inflationary stance and confused about ECB intentions, foreign exchange dealers rushed to sell dollars and buy euros, even as they continued to build up even larger plus positions in Japanese yen. The dollar consequently fell sharply in the foreign exchange markets, while *Bloomberg News* carried forecasts by a number of Wall Street economists predicting a looming spike in U.S. import prices, after five years in which import prices had continuously declined.

Against this background, other disturbing events were unfolding throughout the world.

## Regional Channels and Their Plot Elements

LATIN AMERICA

Within weeks of the turbulence that engulfed the financial markets of the major industrial countries in the spring of 2000, contagion fanned out across Latin America.

In the fallout of the Asian financial and economic meltdown in 1997, Latin America had largely been spared. That would not be the case this time. To be sure, the Russian debt default in 1998 and the subsequent travails of the large U.S. hedge fund, Long Term Capital Management, raised new questions about regional banking systems and foreign currency arrangements. Thus, Brazil had come under pressure in the foreign exchange markets late in 1998, culminating in a steep depreciation of the real, a change at the top of the country's central bank, and some additional policy reforms. But, the stock market in Brazil rebounded smartly and so did other Latin American equity markets. Mexico did especially well. In 1999, the combination of a firmer peso and a spurt of Mexican equity prices generated returns to U.S. dollar-based investors of well over 50 percent. When international markets set back in 2000, though, financial market participants turned their attention to a number of nagging vulnerabilities in the region.

Mexico was in the middle of a hotly contested presidential election when market volatility suddenly escalated. The confi-

dence that Mexico was starting to overcome long-standing banking and economic problems quickly evaporated, and the hesitant
response of the Mexican government, as well as the PRI presidential candidate, did little to reassure domestic and foreign investors. Support for the PAN's candidate picked up, as middle-class
Mexicans told pollsters that there was a pressing need for new
leadership to guide the country through troubled economic
times. The outcome of the election was a virtual dead heat,
with scattered violence at polling places and charges of voting
irregularities by all three political parties. Rumors swirled of a
surge of illegal immigrants seeking to enter the United States.
Correspondents of U.S. and European news organizations who
tried to cover this breaking story were said to have been detained
by the Mexican authorities. The Washington bureaus of the *New
York Times* and CNN revealed that senior members of the House
of Representatives, including both Democrats and Republicans,
had warned the administration not to recognize a winner prema-
turely. Some powerful Republican committee chairs in the U.S.
Senate were even said to be pressing the State Department to
identify the PAN candidate as the victor.

The political drama unfolding in the Mexican election inflamed
already existing passions on the nation's campuses. The more
than year-old stalemate at the National University (UNAM)
flared up again, spreading more forcefully than before to other
Mexican educational institutions and spawning sporadic disor-
der. There were incidents of blockaded highways, some arson,
and scattered gunfire.

A small group of computer hackers siding with the well-armed
radicals and financed by an organization thought to have ties
to associates of Venezuelan President Hugo Chávez had managed to tap into the computers of the second-largest Mexican
bank, possibly with the help of disgruntled employees. It was
the same bank that some months before the onset of global
financial turbulence had completed negotiations for a historic
merger with one of the five leading U.S. banking organizations.
This had been shrilly opposed by a variety of Mexicans, including

those opposed to globalization in general and those who resist tighter links between Mexican and American companies. The hackers published a website displaying a variety of embarrassing data, including detailed information on nonperforming loans that far exceeded the amounts that the Mexican bank had previously disclosed, as well as the numbers of secret accounts controlled by leading political and judicial figures. Mexican financial markets were roiled by reports that the U.S. bank was threatening to withdraw from the merger in view of the leaked information.

The European and Japanese financial authorities judged that Mexico had never honestly come to grips with the bad loans resulting from the 1994–95 financial crisis. While the failed FOBAPROA had been disbanded and replaced by a new institution to deal with troubled bank assets, the Europeans and Japanese foresaw another costly round of banking difficulties. Thus, they took the unprecedented step of demanding a meeting of the IMF's executive board in order to introduce formally a new policy procedure. It would limit the IMF's authority to authorize new loans to a country without obtaining advance approval of the executive board before negotiating terms and conditions. Privately, one European director of the IMF told journalists they were concerned that the United States would attempt to engineer a special loan to Mexico without a thorough appraisal and full consultation with the other G-7 countries, much the way they believed the peso bailout was rammed through in 1995.

Contagion also rippled through South America.

Brazil was bombarded by substantial outflows of funds, including substantial capital flight by Brazilian corporations and wealthy individuals as well as foreign investors. With the currency falling sharply in the foreign exchange markets and therefore threatening to undermine recent progress toward curbing inflation, the Brazilian authorities sought to control the damage. But moderate-size intervention in the foreign exchange market by the central bank had little effect in stemming the depreciation, and it was rumored that the economic team might be asked to resign.

In this deteriorating market situation and to conserve foreign currency reserves for future requirements, Brazil announced that it could no longer continue to service in full its official foreign currency–denominated debt.

The repercussions of renewed financial volatility in Brazil and in the emerging debt markets were felt most urgently in Argentina. While the Argentine peso, tied to the U.S. dollar through its currency board, was dropping along with the dollar against the euro and the Japanese yen, it was surging against the Brazilian real. To many Argentines, the outcome represented the worst of both worlds—large outflows of capital from Argentina combined with an appreciation against the currency of its most important trading partner.

Indeed, already the surge in world oil prices left Venezuela in the strongest financial position in a decade. There were reports that President Chávez was seeking to create a so-called zone of influence in Latin America, financing like-minded soldier-politicians and their personally loyal militias in Bolivia, Ecuador, and Peru. The specter of a less hospitable global economic and financial environment could embolden them to challenge existing governments, many of which had lost considerable public support.

THE GULF

The rise in the price of oil that accelerated following the financial convulsions that began in the spring of 2000 also swelled the dollar foreign exchange reserves of countries in the Gulf, including Saudi Arabia and the United Arab Emirates (UAE). With the U.S. dollar falling sharply in the foreign exchange market and the U.S. bond market remaining volatile and uncertain, the Saudi ambassador to Washington asked for a White House meeting to brief top officials on Saudi thinking on a number of topics.

In his talking points, he explained that with the substantial rebound in oil prices Saudi Arabia was being given the opportunity to play a more activist role in the region. After a decade of periodic conflict, it wanted to explore new and unconventional ways of reducing tensions and possibly establishing greater stability. Accordingly, it was considering a number of departures, some quite bold.

First, it was thinking of building on the precedent of the Israeli-Syrian peace talks by offering Saddam Hussein the chance to rebuild peaceful relations. The Saudi government would be prepared to support ending all current and future U.N. economic sanctions in return for assurances that Iraq would agree to a nonaggression pact with Saudi Arabia.

Second, Saudi Arabia was exploring a parallel reconciliation initiative with Iran. As the initial step, it had drafted the terms of a technical cooperation agreement with Iran to secure shipping lanes in the Gulf.

Third, it was contemplating an indirect channel of communications with Israel to lay the foundation for a process of normalization following the successful completion of the Israeli-Syrian talks. Establishment of a Middle East humanitarian assistance fund, with contributions from all parties, could be proposed at a later stage.

Fourth, it was opening an indirect channel of communications with Islamic groups that have been critical of Saudi involvement with the U.S. military. This may eventually involve some changes in the facilities open to the United States.

As for its financial policy, the ambassador emphasized that Saudi dollar reserves are again more than adequate. Thus, the prudent course would be to sell U.S.-dollar denominated assets and diversify into assets denominated in the euro and yen.

Market sources reported sizable open market sales of U.S. Treasuries by banks normally acting as agent for Mideast governments.

The *Financial Times* broke the news that an Asian financial conglomerate with interests in the United States and Europe had taken material losses in at least its foreign exchange options business and was said to be initiating talks with counterparties to avoid realizing losses. Wealthy Saudi investors are prominent among the owners of the institution.

Reuters news agency carried a report from Bahrain that highly placed individuals in the United Arab Emirates were threatening to withhold the purchase of $8 billion of fighter aircraft, a transaction that had been pending for some time. It quotes market sources that the loss of F-16 sales of such magnitude would be a serious blow to the manufacturer.

TURKEY

The global financial implosion came at a delicate time for Turkey. It had just recently completed negotiations with the IMF for a financing package, but the threat of a significant downturn in global economic activity made it highly unlikely that the tough conditions Turkey agreed to could be met. Turkey informed the IMF staff that it would like to revise them.

Before the staff could respond with the IMF's position, financial circumstances in Turkey took a sudden turn for the worse. More than any other country, Turkey had long depended on the continuing inflows of short-term funds from abroad, both to finance the government's sizable deficit and to provide a major source of liquidity to Turkish banks. Essentially, the funding was rolled over day to day. Sometimes the foreign investor took the foreign exchange rate risk, but at times of heightened tension in global markets, the investors sought to cover their exposures to a faster than anticipated depreciation of the Turkish lira. That effectively shifted the currency risk back onto the banks providing forward foreign exchange facilities.

As the demand for hedging facilities skyrocketed, foreign banks withdrew from the market, leaving Turkish banks as the main counterparties. Foreign investors, rather than routinely rolling over their loans, started to demand their money back. Simultaneously, U.S. financial officials detected unusual activity in the operating accounts of the Turkish central bank normally used to cover payments in and out of the country's foreign currency reserves. After discussion with private-sector sources, it was learned that the central bank had amassed sizable positions in foreign exchange futures and options of its own to camouflage reserve losses.

As this banking crisis unfolded, world attention was fixed on live TV coverage of clashes between Turkish forces and Islamic student demonstrators in Istanbul. The group was protesting arbitrary arrests of student leaders challenging government education policies. In the final police assault, dozens of casualties were apparent.

In the United States, a coalition of human rights groups issued a statement condemning the events. They pledged to pressure congressional delegations to move legislation that would restrict the sale of advanced computers, telecommunications equipment, and military hardware to countries that had a record of human rights abuses. The bill had originally been drafted with China as the target, and it had stalled in a subcommittee. But the latest outburst of public anger encouraged a House subcommittee to pass a version of the bill, even as members of the House and Senate leadership raised doubts whether the measure would be able to come to the floor of either chamber. Turkish parliamentary figures, infuriated by what they viewed as a blatantly anti-Turk provocation, expressed their outrage. Some went so far as to urge the Turkish government to demand the suspension of American military operations from Incrlik airfield.

The *Wall Street Journal* carried an investigative report that exposed a complex scheme by a Turkish-Israeli entity headquartered in the Cayman Islands that had allegedly used insider information to rig trading in a new Internet IPO on the Nasdaq. The IPO had been one of the first to be issued simultaneously in Tel Aviv, Frankfurt, and New York.

EUROPE

At about the same time, EU officials privately requested the U.S. administration to end public statements in favor of early Turkish admittance into the community. While the Turkish candidacy was formally accepted in December 1999, European political leaders were convinced that the country would be unable to meet existing entry criteria for at least ten years and did not want U.S. support to exacerbate what was bound to be a delicate process.

Meanwhile, the continued sell-off of financial assets had its initial spill over onto the German real estate market. It was already reeling from overbuilding in Berlin and elsewhere, a situation that contributed to the collapse of the Holtzmann organization late in 1999. But the turbulence in the world's financial markets tended to draw new attention to the magnitude of office vacancies and other evidence of real estate excesses. In turn, the nonperforming loans of German banks mushroomed. In addition, French, Swiss, and British banks were reported to hold substantial co-investments in the largest real estate ventures.

Opposition to the single currency had been muted during the run-up to the establishment of the euro. In fact, even principled opponents tended to be branded as heretical or even unpatriotic. To illustrate, academics and journalists who felt that the financial and economic consequences would not on balance be positive were excluded from high-level discussions and conferences. However, the outbreak of financial turbulence in the spring of 2000 changed all this. One of the manifestations was the formation of a group called "Concerned economists allied against financial calamity" that included a number of world-renowned scholars, former central bankers, and market practitioners. Their view was that the volatility of the euro was and would remain excessive and that with high levels of unemployment, Europe could not tolerate a period of an unrealistically strong euro. The U.S. embassy in Brussels transmitted a report that two unnamed European governments had asked their legal experts to prepare a memorandum explaining the mechanics of how a country could withdraw from the common currency and reestablish its traditional currency.

## RUSSIA AND EASTERN EUROPE

Russian and German officials helped arrange for meetings that led to a package that included financial infusions into the Russian banking system and a special energy arrangement for Germany. In the deal, a consortium of German banks would buy a special issue of convertible preferred shares offered by the five largest Russian banks. The securities would provide core capital to permit the Russian banks to expand their activities, especially in financing new projects in the energy field. Germany would get a five-year call on Russian oil and natural gas, with strike prices set quarterly at 2 percent below the average world price.

Beset by higher energy prices and the seizing up of international debt markets, Ukraine defaulted on scheduled payments to Russian oil companies. The companies insisted on immediate payment; otherwise, they would be compelled to stop the flow of energy to the country. President Putin also publicly warned his Ukrainian counterpart that any attempt by Ukraine to ration electricity in a way that would lead to discrimination against eastern Ukraine, where large numbers of ethnic Russians reside, would provoke the sternest possible response. President Kuchma instructed his finance minister to seek emergency loans from the IMF and the G-7 to cover the shortfall.

## EAST ASIA

Chinese leaders met in an emergency session to discuss the implications of the global financial crisis for China. Intelligence sources revealed that they decided that the impact would be to worsen the internal financial sector disarray and probably touch off a global economic slowdown that would curb Chinese exports. They also agreed that the process of adapting the Chinese economy to the demands of WTO membership would also produce strains. And in the event that U.S. congressional opponents of normal trading relations between China and the U.S. prevailed, China would face additional difficulties—at least more restricted access to global capital markets. Therefore, it was decided to devalue the renminbi by 35 percent. The public announcement of the action was made on July 1, 2000. Other Asian currency markets reacted sharply.

A further challenge to U.S.-Chinese relations came when Chinese naval officers claimed that Chinese vessels had been fired upon in the vicinity of the Spratly Islands. In the statement, they reserved the right to pursue and apprehend the perpetrators, even if this meant landing troops on one or more of the islands.

Intelligence sources decoded a message from the Chinese to senior Japanese officials explaining the Spratly incident in greater detail and hinting at a possible Chinese-Japanese joint venture to develop oil resources in the area.

A memorandum purportedly written by a junior member of the staff of a newly established international research institute founded by a former high-level bureaucrat was leaked to close associates in the Japanese media. The memo analyzed the potential impact on the Japanese banking system and economy of the global financial turbulence. It called for a new program of "military modernization" to strengthen Japanese capabilities and to provide a buffer against the recurrence of a business recession.

The Japanese Ministry of Finance (MOF) and the Bank of Japan (BOJ) sent a memorandum to their counterparts at the U.S. Treasury and the Federal Reserve to express concern over exchange rate developments. They indicated that Japanese official intervention in the foreign exchange markets had been unsuccessful in restoring stability and that Japan was no longer capable of taking the entire exchange rate risk of its dollar support. Also, the Japanese authorities had been informed that other nations have asked for special foreign currency denominated facilities into which they could convert excess dollars in reserves. Japan would expect to receive, on a most-favored-nation basis, the equivalent or better treatment. In the meantime, in an attempt to offset the deflationary impact of further appreciation in the value of the yen against the dollar, the MOF and BOJ were announcing establishment of a joint study group to analyze the potential policy benefits of imposing a tax on large bank deposits. The so-called negative interest penalty, which would only apply to deposits above 10 million yen, would be designed to discourage speculation in the yen.

Banks from all major countries in the region had sizable exposures with respect to the most serious financial problems that had surfaced since the financial turbulence began.

# Appendix B

# Roundtable on Financial Vulnerabilities: List of Participants and Rapporteur's Report (September 1999)

**Roger M. Kubarych**
*Henry Kaufman Senior Fellow for International Economics and Finance*
Project Director and Moderator

**Céline Gustavson**
Rapporteur

September 29, 1999
11:30 A.M.–5:30 P.M.

## Participants

Henry H. Arnhold
*Arnhold and S. Bleichroeder, Inc.*

Kenneth D. Balick
*Nomura Capital*

Caroline Baum
*Bloomberg*

Brandon Becker
*Wilmer Cutler & Pickering*

David O. Beim
*Columbia University*

Rhett Brandon
*Simpson Thacher & Bartlett*

Robert E. Denham
*Munger, Tolles & Olson*

David A. Duffié
*USN Military Fellow, 1999–2000*
*Council on Foreign Relations*

Benjamin M. Friedman
*Harvard University*

Robert R. Glauber
*Harvard University*

Richard K. Goeltz
*American Express Company*

Martin Gross
*Sandalwood Securities, Inc.*

Céline Gustavson
*Council on Foreign Relations*

John G. Heimann
*Financial Stability Institute*

John B. Hurford
*Credit Suisse Asset Management*

Lawrence J. Korb
*Council on Foreign Relations*

Roger M. Kubarych
*Council on Foreign Relations*

Stanley McChrystal
*USA Military Fellow, 1999–2000*
*Council on Foreign Relations*

Kim McKenzie
*USAF Military Fellow, 1999–2000*
*Council on Foreign Relations*

Floyd Norris
*The New York Times*

John J. Phelan Jr.
*Chairman Emeritus, NYSE*

Beatrice E. Rangel-Mantilla
*Cisneros Group of Companies*

John J. Roberts
*American International Group, Inc.*

Gideon Rose
*Council on Foreign Relations*

Daniele Rulli
*Fiat USA, Inc.*

Richard E. Salomon
*Spears, Benzak, Salomon & Farrell, Inc.*

Frank Savage
*Alliance Capital Management International*

Robert J. Shiller
*Yale University*

Martin Shubik
*Yale School of Management*

Benn Steil
*Council on Foreign Relations*

Richard Sylla
*New York University*

Marina v.N. Whitman
*University of Michigan*

Guy P. Wyser-Pratte
*Wyser-Pratte & Co.*

Noriyasu Yamada
*JETRO New York*

Fareed Zakaria
*Foreign Affairs*

Ezra K. Zilkha
*Zilkha & Sons*

## Rapporteur's Report

The Council on Foreign Relations has established a new research program that will examine the linkages between the financial markets and broader economic, foreign policy, and national security concerns. The Roundtable on Financial Vulnerabilities was the first part of a three-part series on the complex policy problems that a potential financial crisis sometime in the future might raise. The purpose of the series is to develop research findings and expert advice that policymakers can use to help prepare for an unexpected financial mishap and perhaps take steps to mitigate its adverse consequences. Our premise is that perhaps the most dangerous near-term threat to U.S. world leadership, and thus indirectly to U.S. security, would be a sharp decline in the U.S. securities markets that touched off a worldwide financial disturbance. It would likely stun the U.S. economy at a time when the strength of the U.S. economy is critical to the economic prosperity and financial health of other nations, their political stability, and ultimately international security.

Thirty-six individuals, including market practitioners, scholars, and former government officials, participated in the roundtable. Roger Kubarych was the moderator. The roundtable had two objectives. The first was to review the lessons learned from past stock market breaks and other financial disturbances as well as from the policy responses to them. The second was to identify vulnerabilities in the current economic and financial situation that could at some point challenge the generally favorable conditions that now prevail. (A third objective—to begin developing elements of a hypothetical scenario in which these favorable conditions would meet a significant challenge—was taken up at a subsequent meeting of foreign policy and market experts on October 20.) The following is a brief summary that highlights the lively and insightful discussion that ensued.

## Lessons from Past Financial Disturbances

The roundtable began with the participants outlining the lessons learned from past financial disturbances. One of the primary lessons is that virtually every major financial crisis since the 1970s has been a liquidity crisis. In the late 1960s, by contrast, technical deficiencies were sources of occasional mishaps. A progressive escalation of transactions volume, in part a reflection of the unprecedented buildup of private pension funds, state and local retirement funds, and other institutional investor activity, strained then-existing infrastructure on the leading exchanges. Moreover, new methods of managing portfolios came to the fore that greatly enlarged turnover. This surge in transactions volume overwhelmed the archaic system that had been in place since the early 1920s and led ultimately to sweeping changes in the structure and composition of the marketplace. These problems had already been smoldering by the time the stock market faltered in 1973–74, a period of great political and economic upheaval in the wake of the Vietnam War disengagement, the OPEC oil shock, and the outbreak of high levels of inflation. This moved everyone, including the banks, member firms, and exchanges, to put new systems and mechanisms into place. Subsequently, upgrades to the technology of the trading system were continuously demanded and implemented reasonably successfully.

Nevertheless, fragilities in the markets—currency, fixed-income, commodities, as well as equities—came to the surface with great regularity, almost every three years or so. The common denominator was the sudden loss of liquidity of troubled financial institutions or entire markets that was a causal factor in every subsequent crisis, whether it was the silver crisis of the early 1980s, the Drysdale incident, the sharp plunge in equity prices in 1987, or the 1998 near-collapse of a major hedge fund, Long Term Capital Management (LTCM).

A crucial lesson of these recurrent financial disturbances is that liquidity should not be withdrawn—at the domestic or international level—in times of crisis. Indeed, all roundtable participants concurred that it is essential to infuse abundant liquidity into the system. Or as John Phelan put it, it is essential to "put water wings under the market and get it back up again." That is what got the system through the 1987 and 1998 crises with minimal damage to the financial system at large.

Another key lesson is that the fragmentation of financial regulatory mechanisms can make it more difficult to deal effectively with an imminent financial crisis. The United States has a complex system of financial supervisions and regulation, with overlapping authority in several areas but with important participants left out of the supervisory net altogether. But however complicated the U.S. approach, it does have considerable talent and technical know-how. By contrast, financial regulatory mechanisms in the rest of the world lag far behind those in the United States. Many countries—particularly in the emerging markets—will have a very difficult time dealing with the economic, financial, and political consequences of a future financial crisis because they often have weak institutions that are ill-equipped to deal with complex effects of financial disturbances. While financial squalls in small or medium-size developing countries may not have an impact on the United States right away, a future crisis that raged through an entire region could ultimately have a dramatic impact on the economies of the United States and other major industrial countries. Moreover, even if the adverse impact is muted, there will still be pressure on the United States to keep the affected countries afloat because many U.S. companies may be dependent on their markets. Similar pressures will be felt by governments in Europe and Japan from their companies.

The sudden seizing up of liquidity is one common denominator of past disturbances. The second is the existence of what might be called accelerators. They are a mixture of technical and behavioral factors within the financial system that tend to accelerate the decline of asset prices once some trigger sets it off. In the case of the United States, one of the important lessons that was learned from the 1987 stock market break is not that the market went down, but that it went down so fast—because of the impact of powerful, but not easily foreseen factors that *accelerated* its decline. Participants in the roundtable compiled a lengthy list of accelerators. One of the most important was leverage—the direct or indirect use of borrowed funds by market participants to enlarge their exposure to market movements. For example, in the 1987 episode, no one had a detailed knowledge of how much leverage there was in the system, what forms it took, who ultimately bore the risks involved, how much risk was hedged, and how reliable those hedges would prove to be. At that time, markets in financial derivatives were developing rapidly, but there was little appreciation of how those markets would behave at a time of stress. Several roundtable participants agreed that today "there is more leverage and less information about it than ever." Greater *transparency*, through enhanced data collection and dissemination, is essential to ensuring that the central banks will be in a position to provide liquidity promptly and to the right institutions to contain some future financial crisis.

A second accelerator was what might be called forced selling, or involuntary liquidation of equity, bond, currency, or commodity positions. Forced selling has been a recurring theme in many past financial crises. In 1929, forced selling was prevalent in the retail markets because of margin calls. In 1987, it took the form of portfolio insurance, which was a superficially water-tight (but ultimately failed) method of protecting against stock market losses through selling of shares at successively lower prices. In 1998, it was evident in the unwinding of purportedly hedged positions in which exposures turned out after the fact to be additive rather than offsetting.

The concept of forced selling can encompass a number of behaviors. For instance, it can reflect the operation of various kinds of trend-following or momentum-based trading systems, in which computers are programmed to issue sell signals to investment managers when the market falls. Forced selling can result from the application of so-called value at risk and similar kinds of statistical models, which large banks and other prominent financial institutions use to control their trading risks. Mutual funds can be subject to a kind of forced selling in response to withdrawals by their investors. Bond managers can be forced to sell fixed-income securities when the credit rating of an issuer is downgraded to below what clients have authorized. Or the concept can be applied to the kind of self-imposed forced selling: people do it because they think a drop in the market will go on for a long time and fear that their securities are going to go down in price.

Generally, history suggests that no single factor will cause a market to go wrong, or act as an accelerator once something has gone wrong. Rather, it is the interplay between several factors, including leverage, herd mentality, and the lack of faith in buffer mechanisms, that creates a systemic problem.

A consistent feature of the crises the roundtable reviewed was that each resulted from a weakness in the market structure at that particular point in time. Yet, the important point was that the particular weakness was only identified in hindsight. Ironically, in some ways we are lucky that there has been a crisis every four to five years, because that has enabled officials and market participants to identify the existing weaknesses and try to fix them before they metastasized. Not enough work is ever done to identify the inconsistencies and fragilities in the markets before a crisis happens, because of the natural human tendency to believe that "this time will be different." That is seldom true.

## Vulnerabilities in the Structure of Financial Markets

The second part of the discussion focused on vulnerabilities in the present economic and financial setting that may at some point pose a threat to market stability. "The four most dangerous words," one practitioner suggested, "are 'it's different this time.'" Indeed, several participants agreed that the complacency that has accompanied the rise of the stock market in the United States, and the associated belief that old problems are no longer relevant (such as the danger of a potential revival of inflation), is an enormous problem. Vulnerabilities do exist, however, although they are not equally worrisome and several are capable of being dealt with prospectively. The following summarizes the widely varying concerns of roundtable participants.

1. There is a danger that far more people have invested in the system than in the past, either through mutual funds or directly in the market, and many of these people are doing it with money they cannot afford to lose because they will need it for their retirement.

2. Complacency injects a real vulnerability. Nowadays, the markets seem to bounce back every time they encounter turbulence. As a result, everybody thinks everything is okay: The United States, with a strong economy, low inflation, and political stability, is fine. Europe is coming along. Japan is putting its financial problems behind it and will gradually pick up economic momentum. Many debt-troubled countries in Asia and elsewhere are beginning to get an economic rebound. In this pleasant environment, any event that triggers an abrupt sell-off in one or another of the leading financial markets could have a serious impact on investor confidence, if it is not reversed quickly.

3. Because there are no international regulatory mechanisms, accounting standards, trading standards, or agreed disclosure principles, this would put the whole fabric of world financial markets at considerable risk, particularly as globalization continues to increase the links between countries and financial markets.

4. Even the most broadly accepted policy prescriptions can go awry. It was remarked that "governments are political in the final analysis."

5. Financial systems in the non-G-10 countries are broke, and accounting standards and regulatory policies in these countries also lag far behind and will need years to recover.

6. The kind of collective psychology that in times past precipitated bank runs now readily triggers contagion among securitized financial markets.

7.  For those emerging markets that still do not have well-developed capital markets, there is no alternative to their banking systems for creating credit needed to support adequate economic growth. However, banking systems in a large number of developing countries remain extremely weak.

8.  Notwithstanding the lessons learned from the devastating problems encountered by LTCM and other highly exposed institutional investors, leverage in the marketplace is still large although not well measured or monitored.

9.  There is a basic moral hazard at work in the markets, namely that the Federal Reserve and the other major central banks will always be prepared to provide sufficient liquidity to prevent an incipient financial crisis from widening. They also are expected to continue to be the lender of last resort for a large number of financial institutions other than the traditional commercial banks that were their traditional mandate. Put another way, more and more participants are deemed to be "too big to fail" whether or not they are banks.

10. Neither private economists nor those working in central banks or finance ministries are able to use historical data to determine how so-called wealth effects will evolve in the next financial disturbance. Wide differences of opinion exist among analysts on this controversial topic.

11. Equity markets have elements of vulnerability when calibrated by conventional yardsticks, such as price-earnings ratios, dividend yields, or stock market capitalization as a percentage of GDP.

Not all participants put the dangers of a stock market correction at the top of their list of concerns. One view is that a break in stock prices would have less impact at the macro-level than most people think. The argument is that wealth effects are not as important as commonly thought and that in any case consumer expenditures do not appear to be tightly related to stock market performance. The typical consumer today is still spending as if stock prices were the same as two years ago, rather than current, much higher levels. The reason for this is that although stock market ownership is broader, the vehicles of this ownership—401(k)'s, for example—do not lend themselves to supporting current consumer spending.

Nevertheless, even a number of participants were concerned that after seventeen years of mostly rising share prices and the corresponding erosion in the personal savings rate to almost zero, a drop in asset prices could have an asymmetric and there-fore quicker constraining effect on the level of consumption expenditures than might be predicted on the basis of the lagged response to rises in asset prices. Consequently, a dramatic decline in asset prices would be likely to have a significant and reason-ably prompt adverse impact on the economy.

What would be worse is if the Federal Reserve and other major central banks were constrained in their ability to inject liquidity in order to cushion such an adverse economic impact. There was a widely held belief that the Federal Reserve could routinely bail the United States and indeed the world economy out of any predic-ament. The result was not improbable. But that degree of confi-dence in the efficacy of monetary policy as an antidote to a financial crisis is excessive. That overconfidence is a factor that many round-table participants cited as a moral hazard, and hence a vulnerabil-ity, in the current environment. Still, several participants felt it would take a lot to scare individuals out of the stock market, because the average person is invested for the long term. How-ever, it was acknowledged that if a decline in asset prices took place over a long period of time as in the 1970s, rather than taking the form of a sudden drop that was soon reversed, as in 1987, the effect might be such that individuals would begin to pull out of the market en masse.

Moreover, a broader financial disturbance than just a decline in the value of the stock market, for example through a sharp drop in real estate prices, could have substantial macroeconomic repercussions. While there was disagreement over whether that specific risk is an immediate danger, given the spotty behavior of at least commercial real estate prices lately, participants largely agreed that an exogenous factor or factors could trigger a downturn in the financial markets substantial enough to have severe adverse economic consequences.

One such exogenous factor would be the failure of a significant portion of the global banking system, especially in the emerging markets. One analyst specializing in this field believes that as a source of vulnerability the prospect of systemic bank failures dwarfs the other issues. The reason is that the level of banking failures in the recent past, both in the United States and around the world, is unprecedented. While there were very few bank failures in the United States and in most countries between the 1930s and 1970, that number rose exponentially during the 1970s and 1980s. A World Bank study for the years 1970 to 1995 showed that there were 127 bank failures in ninety-four countries during that time span, in which all or substantially all of the banking capital was exhausted. Consequently, the cost of resolving these failures has escalated as well. The cost of the banking failure in Indonesia in 1998, for example, has been calculated at 130 percent of GDP. Indeed, banks in many countries are broke, despite the appearance—created through artificial means, such as conveniently changing accounting methods—that they are not. And even in the case of countries where safety nets exist, the question becomes whether these safety nets will work a second time, particularly if nothing is done to deal with the problems that created the conditions for failing banks in the first place.

A second exogenous factor, which several of the participants agreed could become a serious vulnerability, was the relative strength of the dollar, which one participant predicted would act as a binding constraint on the ability of the Federal Reserve to infuse the financial system with abundant liquidity during a prospective financial disturbance. Up to now, the depreciation of the dollar has been limited to the Japanese yen. Given the strength of Japan's international trade position and given that the dollar has been appreciating with respect to the euro, the equity and bond markets have not been affected. However, should the dollar begin to go down against the euro, this could act as an important—and worrisome—trigger for a downturn in the financial markets and eventually in the U.S. economy.

A third and related exogenous factor that was highlighted as a potential vulnerability is a further sharp rise in the price of oil and its impact on the strength of the dollar. Significantly, and contrary to many predictions, the price of oil has already risen dramatically from $11 a barrel in February to $25 in September. [As of early November, it had settled back to about $22 a barrel.] This was largely the result of political events: the election of Hugo Chávez in Venezuela, who stopped the country's practice of exceeding its OPEC quota, and the decision by Mexico to cooperate with OPEC in production and pricing strategy.

## Preventing Financial Crises vs. Dealing with Their Consequences

The question of prevention versus crisis management as a means to deal with economic and financial disturbances generated considerable controversy and a clash of strong views. Financial crises can be costly, but so can undertaking preventive measures that cause undesirable side effects by inhibiting market innovation and risk-taking. It is important to recognize that the authorities may choose to do nothing, not because of disinterest but because they perceive that the costs of doing something outweigh the likely benefits. Consequently, it is worth considering mainly those preventive measures that are less intrusive, and less costly, such as enforcing disclosure and transparency as a means of trying to protect people from making bad decisions, as well as trying to maximize the possibility of good decisions.

As one roundtable participant put it, in speaking about prevention, it is important to know what you are trying to prevent: a significant decline in financial markets or overshooting.

Although policy measures may not be able to prevent overshooting outright, much more needs to be done in the realm of public policy to examine what can be done to reduce the adverse consequences overshooting does have. For example, through public policy measures, liquidity can be injected into the system to discourage a herd mentality in which everyone seeks to get out of the market at the same time. Moreover, a system can be instituted that will monitor the solvency of the major market players to guard against excessive leverage. Also, public policy can affect market regulation to maintain orderly markets during periods of rapid adjustment to events and the characteristically high volatility associated with such adjustments.

One thing that was true in 1987 and 1998 remains true today: anything that will happen in the market will happen quickly. This puts the burden on the regulatory system to be able to respond just as quickly. There are weaknesses in the regulatory structure today, however, that would interfere with the ability of regulators to deal with a crisis in real time. The regulatory system is fragmented: banks are regulated one way, investment banks another, futures are regulated by the Commodity Futures Trading Commission (CFTC), securities are regulated by the Securities and Exchange Commission (SEC), and no one knows what positions hedge funds and other highly leveraged institutional investors have on a real time basis. In a time of crisis, these regulators would have to be able to coordinate successfully among themselves, which, even with the best of intentions, is not likely to happen quickly enough, if it happens at all. This weakness in the system of financial supervision and regulation can be improved upon.

In sum, perfect prevention of future financial disturbances is unattainable and unwise. But a sequence of what might be thought of as small steps, such as harmonizing the fragmented structure of supervision of banking, insurance, securities, and unregulated financial institutions at the domestic and international level, or having more explicit supervisory standards for securitized financial markets and markets for financial derivatives, could put us on a path toward prevention. For instance, controls on position-taking by hedge funds would be deemed as entirely too intrusive, but getting more information on the degree of leverage being deployed by such investors might be acceptable—and would be helpful at the time of a market disturbance. It is not the role of public policy to intervene to dictate behavior to participants in private markets but rather simply to warn of the risks that are being taken.

# Appendix C

# Scenario-Building Roundtable: List of Participants (October 1999)

**Roger M. Kubarych**
*Henry Kaufman Senior Fellow for International Economics and Finance*
Moderator

Wednesday, October 20, 1999
4:00–6:00 P.M.

### Participants

Elizabeth Allan
*Scudder Kemper Investments, Inc.*

Jack David

Hans W. Decker
*Siemens Corporation*

Logan D. Delany, Jr.
*Delany Capital Management Corp.*

David A. Duffie
*USN Military Fellow, 1999–2000
Council on Foreign Relations*

Hani K. Findakly
*Potomac Capital*

Céline Gustavson
*Council on Foreign Relations*

Theresa A. Havell
*Havell Capital Management*

Paul Heer
*Council on Foreign Relations*

David Kellogg
*Council on Foreign Relations*

Marc Levinson
*Chase Securities Inc.*

Anne R. Luzzatto
*Council on Foreign Relations*

Walter Mead
*Council on Foreign Relations*

Elie Ofek
*New York University*

Gideon Rose
*Council on Foreign Relations*

Sherle R. Schwenninger
*Council on Foreign Relations*

Richard Sylla
*New York University*

John H. Watts
*Fischer Francis Trees & Watts*

Guy P. Wyser-Pratte
*Wyser-Pratte & Co.*

Fareed Zakaria
*Foreign Affairs*

# Appendix D

# Simulation Participants (January 2000)

**Roger M. Kubarych**
*Henry Kaufman Senior Fellow for International Economics and Finance*
Project Director

**Capt. David A. Duffié**
*USN Military Fellow, 1999–2000*
Assistant Director

**Andrew Hilton**
*Centre for the Study of Financial Innovation*
Commentator

**David Shirreff\***
*Euromoney*
Commentator

January 22, 2000

---

\*Shirreff wrote a blow-by-blow description of what he was able to observe during the simulation in the March 2000 issue of *Euromoney* magazine under the headline "U.S. Experts Play at Global Meltdown." He admitted that he was handicapped by not being able to listen in on all five groups simultaneously, but he faithfully conveyed the sense of activity and time pressure that all participants felt.

## Participants*

### Decision-Makers Group

Moderator: Marc Levinson, *Chase Securities Inc. (Chief of Staff)*
Council Staff: Leah Scholer
Observer: Jerome Jacobson, *Economic Studies, Inc.*

Mario Baeza
*TCW/Latin America Partners, LLC*
(Secretary of the Treasury)

Kathy Finn Bloomgarden
*Ruder Finn*
(House of Representatives)

Tom Donahue
*Work in America Institute*
(White House Political
Adviser)

Robert Hormats
*Goldman, Sachs & Co.*
(House of Representatives)

James Jones
*Manatt, Phelps, and Phillips, LLP*
(National Security Adviser)

Brian Kenny
*W.R. Grace & Co.*
(Senate)

John A. Levin
*John A. Levin & Company, Inc.*
(Senate)

Peter G. Peterson
*The Blackstone Group*
(White House International
Economic Adviser)

Richard Ravitch
*Ravitch, Rice & Co.*
(House of Representatives)

John Whitehead
*AEA Investors, Inc.*
(Secretary of State)

R. James Woolsey
*Shea & Gardner*
(Secretary of Defense)

---

*Participants in the Decision-Makers Group were asked to play specific roles. These are underlined and listed after their names. Members of the other groups were not asked to play specific roles, with the exception of the moderator of the Central Banking Group.

## Central Banking Group

Moderator: John Heimann, *Financial Stability Institute (Head of the Federal Reserve)*
Rapporteur: Deborah Burand, *U.S Department of the Treasury*
Council Staff: Negar Katirai

Elizabeth Allan
*Scudder Kemper Investments, Inc.*

Derrick Cephas
*Cadwalader, Wickersham & Taft*

Sam Y. Cross
*Columbia University*

Jessica Einhorn

Peter Fisher
*Federal Reserve Bank of New York*

Benjamin Friedman
*Harvard University*

Bevis Longstreth
*Debevoise & Plimpton*

Martin Mayer
*Brookings Institution*

Walter Russell Mead
*Council on Foreign Relations*

Scott Pardee
*Middlebury College*

Robert Solomon
*Brookings Institution*

## Financial Regulatory Group

Moderator: Robert Carswell, *Shearman & Sterling*
Rapporteur: Melvin Williams, *Salomon Smith Barney*
Council Staff: Veronique Aubert

Brandon Becker
*Wilmer, Cutler and Pickering*

Robert Denham
*Munder, Tolles and Olson*

George Hoguet
*State Street Global Advisors*

Edward Kwalwasser
*New York Stock Exchange*

Roger Leeds
*Johns Hopkins University School of Advanced International Studies*

Ernie Patrikis
*American International Group*

Hal Scott
*Harvard Law School*

Benn Steil
*Council on Foreign Relations*

Edward Waitzer
*Stikeman, Elliott*

Tatsuo Watanabe
*Japanese Ministry of Finance*

## Economics and Trade Group

Moderator: Richard Goeltz, *American Express Company*
Rapporteur: Nicholas Beim, *Goldman, Sachs & Co.*
Council Staff: Harpreet Mann

Nicholas A. Bratt
*Scudder Kemper Investments, Inc.*

Hans Decker
*Columbia University*

Hani Findakly
*Potomac Capital*

David Hale
*Zurich Kemper*

Gary Horlick
*O'Melveny & Myers*

Yves Andre Istel
*Rothschild, Inc.*

Merit Janow
*Columbia University*

Andrew Kim
*Sit/Kim International Investment
Associates, Inc.*

Charles Levy
*Wilmer, Cutler & Pickering*

Omatunde Mahoney
*International Asset Management*

Irene Meister
*Irene Meister & Associates*

Nancy Newcomb
*Citicorp*

Seamus O'Cleireacain
*Columbia University*

Gerald A. Pollack

Bruce Stokes
*Council on Foreign Relations*

Alan Wm. Wolff
*Dewey Ballantine*

## Foreign Policy and National Security Group

Moderator: William Clark, *The Japan Society*
Rapporteur: Cynthia Tindell, *GE Capital Services*
Council Staff: Rob Thomson

Diego Arria
*The Columbus Group*

Richard Betts
*Columbia University*

Jack David

Richard Gardner
*Morgan, Lewis & Bockius*

David Gordon
*National Intelligence Council*

Martin Gross
*Sandalwood Securities*

Charles Heck
*Trilateral Commission*

Robert Helander
*Kaye, Scholer, Fierman, Hays &
Handler*

Lawrence Korb
*Council on Foreign Relations*

Gideon Rose
*Council on Foreign Relations*

Maurice Sonnenberg

Gordon Stewart
*Insurance Information Institute*

Bernard Trainor
*Council on Foreign Relations,
Washington, D.C.*

Guy Wyser-Pratte
*Wyser-Pratte & Co.*

Fareed Zakaria
*Foreign Affairs*

# *Appendix E*

# Charts of Movements in Financial Variables during the Simulation

# Dow Jones Industrial Average
*(Actual and Hypothetical)*

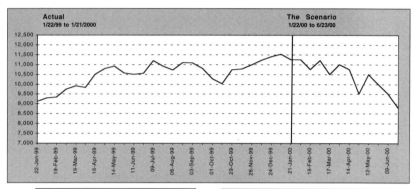

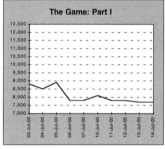

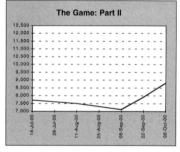

# Nasdaq Composite
*(Actual and Hypothetical)*

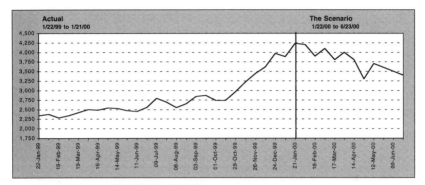

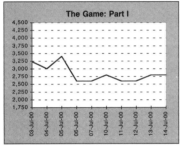

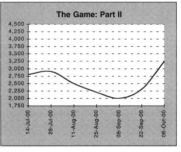

# Nikkei 225
## *(Actual and Hypothetical)*

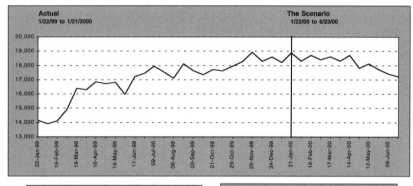

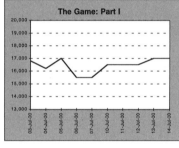

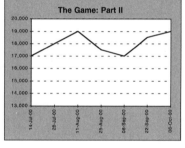

# DAX
## (Actual and Hypothetical)

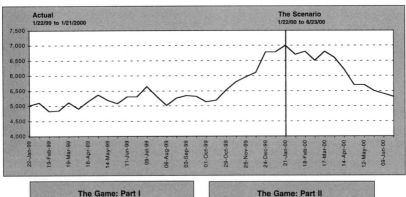

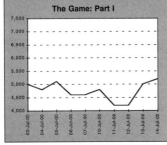

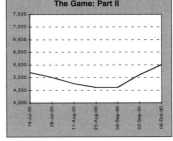

# Value of Yen in Dollar Terms
## *(Actual and Hypothetical)*

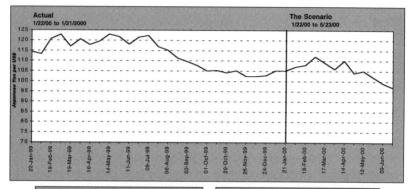

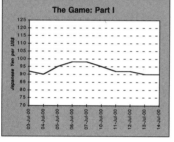

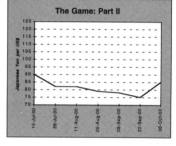

# Value of Euro in Dollar Terms
*(Actual and Hypothetical)*

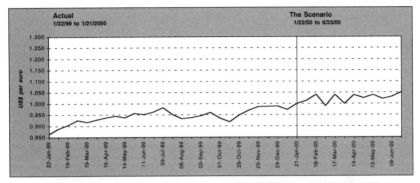

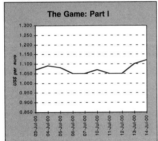

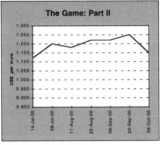

# Yield to Maturity of Thirty-Year U.S. Treasury Bond
## (*Actual and Hypothetical*)

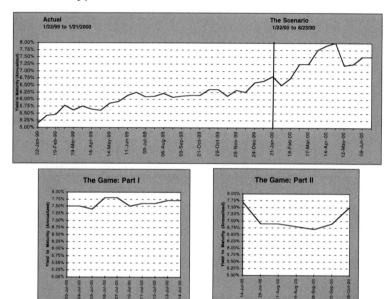

# WTI Price of Crude Oil
## *(Actual and Hypothetical)*

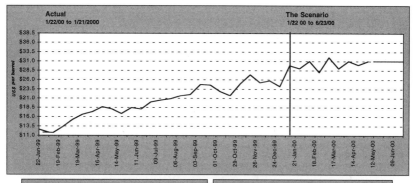

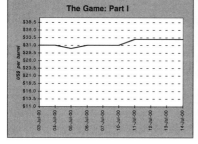

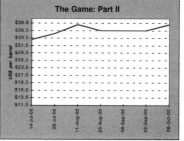

# Appendix F

# New York Conference Agenda (July 2000)

The Next Financial Crisis:
Warning Signs, Damage Control,
and Impact

July 12–13, 2000

Conference Directors:

**David Kellogg**
*Vice President, Corporate Affairs*

**Roger Kubarych**
*Henry Kaufman Senior Fellow for International
Economics and Finance*

### Corporate Sponsors

Barclays Capital                    Tyco International, Ltd.

### Table Sponsors

AEA Investors Inc.

Alliance Capital Management,
L.P.

American International Group,
Inc.

American Securities, L.P.

Banco Santander Central
Hispano

The Blackstone Group

BP-Amoco

Credit Suisse First Boston

*Dresdner Kleinwort Benson*

*FleetBoston Financial*

*GE Capital Services, Inc.*

*Lehman Brothers*

*Morgan Stanley Dean Witter & Co.*

*NatWest Group*

*PaineWebber*

*Patricof & Co. Ventures, Inc.*

*Standard Chartered Bank*

*Xerox Corporation*

## Conference Program

### Wednesday, July 12, 2000

11:00–12:00 P.M.    REGISTRATION

12:00–1:40 P.M.    LUNCHEON
IT'S THE FINANCIAL MARKETS, STUPID! A DIALOGUE
WITH HANNES ANDROSCH AND HENRY KAUFMAN
*How is the current "marketized" environment
different from past eras? In this new environment, are
markets even more prone to excesses that lead to
instability? Does this instability create new
complications for foreign policy and national security?
What can be done?*

**Hannes Androsch,** Chair, Androsch International
Management Consulting; former Vice
Chancellor of Austria
**Henry Kaufman,** President, Henry Kaufman and
Company, Inc.
*Presider:* **Leslie H. Gelb,** President, Council on
Foreign Relations

1:40–2:20 P.M.    BREAK

2:20–3:20 P.M.    STRESS TESTING THE SYSTEM
WAR-GAMING THE NEXT FINANCIAL CRISIS:
LEARNING FROM THE COUNCIL'S POLICY SIMULATION

**Jessica Einhorn,** former Managing Director, the
World Bank

**James R. Jones,** Senior Counsel, Manatt, Phelps & Phillips; former Chair and CEO, American Stock Exchange

*Presider:* **Roger M. Kubarych,** Henry Kaufman Senior Fellow for International Economics and Finance, Council on Foreign Relations

3:20–3:40 P.M.    BREAK

3:40–4:40 P.M.    BREAKOUT SESSIONS I: WARNING SIGNS AND DAMAGE CONTROL
FINANCIAL, ECONOMIC, AND POLITICAL STRESS TESTING

Participants will attend one of the four Regional Breakout Groups *or* the Workshop on Scenario Building and Simulations

A.  **Regional and Country Breakout Groups:**
*What are the regional and country vulnerabilities and pressure points? What are the implications?*

I.  **China**

**Robert S. Ross,** Professor, Harvard University, Fairbank Center for East Asian Research
**Donald Roth,** Managing Partner, Emerging Markets Partnership
*Presider:* **Winston Lord,** former Assistant Secretary of State for East Asian and Pacific Affairs; former U.S. Ambassador to China

II.  **Latin America**

**Lacey Gallagher,** Director, Latin America Economies, Credit Suisse First Boston Corporation
**Martin Schubert,** Chair, the Eurinam Group
*Presider:* **Brian O'Neill,** Managing Director and Chair, Latin America, the Chase Manhattan Corporation

III.  **South Asia**

**Punita Kumar-Sinha,** Senior Portfolio Manager and Executive Director, CIBC Oppenheimer
**David Unger,** Editorial Board, the *New York Times*
*Presider:* **Robert J. Pelosky,** Managing Director, Morgan Stanley Dean Witter & Co.

IV. **Sub-Saharan Africa**

> **Kwesi Botchwey,** Director of Africa Research and Programs, Center for International Development, Harvard University; former Minister of Finance, Republic of Ghana
> **Brian C. McK. Henderson,** Senior Vice President, Merrill Lynch International, Inc.
> *Presider:* **Vincent Mai,** Chair, AEA Investors Inc.

B. **Workshop on Scenario Building and Simulations**
   *A practical guide for designing and using simulation as a tool for improved risk-management and strategic planning*

> **William J. Flanagan,** Senior Managing Director, Cantor Fitzgerald
> **Peter Schwartz,** Chair, Global Business Network; former head of scenario planning at Royal Dutch/Shell
> *Presider:* **David A. Duffié,** USN Military Fellow 1999–2000, Council on Foreign Relations

| | |
|---|---|
| 4:40–5:10 P.M. | BREAK |
| 5:10–6:10 P.M. | BREAKOUT SESSIONS II: WARNING SIGNS AND DAMAGE CONTROL FINANCIAL, ECONOMIC, AND POLITICAL STRESS TESTING Participants will attend one of the four Regional Breakout Groups *or* the Workshop on Scenario Building and Simulations |

A. **Regional and Country Breakout Groups:**
   *What are the regional and country vulnerabilities and pressure points? What are the implications?*

I. **Europe and Russia**

> **Scott Horton,** Senior Partner, Patterson, Belknap, Webb & Tyler
> **Heiko Thieme,** Chair and President, American Heritage Management Corporation
> **Martin Walker,** Public Policy Fellow, Woodrow Wilson International Center for Scholars
> *Presider:* **Charles A. Kupchan,** Whitney H. Shepardson Fellow and Director, European Studies, Council on Foreign Relations

## II. Japan

**Gerry Curtis,** Professor of Political Science, Columbia University
**Kathleen R. Flaherty,** President and Chief Operating Officer, Winstar International
*Presider:* **Bernard Wysocki,** Economic News Editor, the *Wall Street Journal*

## III. North Africa and the Middle East

**Mohammed Abalkhail,** former Minister of Finance and National Economy, Kingdom of Saudi Arabia
**Frank Savage,** Chair, Alliance Capital Management International
*Presider:* **Edward Djerejian,** Director, James A. Baker III Institute for Public Policy of Rice University; former Assistant Secretary of State for Near Eastern Affairs; former U.S. Ambassador to Israel and the Syrian Arab Republic

## IV. Southeast Asia

**Kishore Mahbubani,** Ambassador, Permanent Mission of the Republic of Singapore to the United Nations
**Tien-Yu Sieh,** Senior Vice President and Equity Portfolio Manager, Scudder Kemper Investments, Inc.
**Dov Zakheim,** Chief Executive Officer, SPC International Corporation
*Presider:* **Kathryn Pilgrim,** Anchor/Correspondent, CNN

## B. Workshop on Scenario Building and Simulations
*A practical guide for designing and using simulation as a tool for improved risk-management and strategic planning*

**Peter Schwartz,** Chair, Global Business Network; former head of scenario planning at Royal Dutch/Shell
*Presider:* **David Gordon,** National Intelligence Officer, National Intelligence Council

6:30–7:30 P.M.   COCKTAIL RECEPTION AT THE YALE CLUB

7:30–9:00 P.M.   DINNER AT THE YALE CLUB
*How to improve decision-making in an increasingly complex global system*

*Keynote Speaker:* **Alan Greenspan,** Chair, Board of Governors of the Federal Reserve System
*Introduction by:* **Peter G. Peterson,** Chair, the Blackstone Group; Chairman, Council on Foreign Relations

## Thursday, July 13, 2000

8:00–8:30 A.M.   CONTINENTAL BREAKFAST

8:30–10:00 A.M.   A THREE-WAY DEBATE: HIGH-TECH BUBBLE—OR NOT?
- *Yes, and when it bursts, it will bring down the rest of the market.*
  **Robert Shiller,** Stanley B. Resor Professor of Economics, Cowles Foundation, Yale University

- *Yes, but the market at large can absorb the shock.*
  **Craig Drill,** Chair and CEO, Craig Drill Partners

- *No, it's a precursor of better things to come for the market at large.*
  **Lawrence Kudlow,** Chief U.S. Economist and Investment Strategist, ING Barings

*Presider:* **Robert D. Hormats,** Vice Chair, Goldman Sachs International; former Assistant Secretary of State for Economic and Business Affairs

10:00–10:30 A.M.   BREAK

10:30–11:45 A.M.   WORST CASE SCENARIO: ANOTHER 1987-LIKE MARKET BREAK? WHAT MIGHT BE THE ECONOMIC AND POLITICAL BACKLASH?
*Will Main Street stick with Wall Street in the next financial crisis? How will the public respond given the greater participation of average investors in the markets? Will there be a political backlash? What could be done to deal with the markets, possible lawsuits, and political reaction? Is the international spread of an equity culture at risk?*

**John J. Brennan,** Chair and CEO, the Vanguard Group, Inc.

**James Grant,** Editor, *Grant's Interest Rate Observer*
*Presider:* **George J.W. Goodman,** Chair and CEO,
   Adam Smith Global Television

11:45–12:15 P.M.    **BREAK**

12:15–2:00 P.M.    **LUNCHEON**
**LOOKING BEYOND NEAR-TERM VULNERABILITIES: THE
NEXT MARKET DRIVERS**
*What will be the next compelling investment story?
Can information technology continue to lead the
financial markets? Or will exciting advances in human
genome science, robotics, or other technologies move to
the fore?*

**Ray Kurzweil,** Inventor, entrepreneur, and author
   of *The Age of Spiritual Machines*
*Presider:* **Maurice R. Greenberg,** Chair and CEO,
   American International Group, Inc.; Vice
   Chairman, Council on Foreign Relations

# Appendix G

# Chicago Simulation Participants and Summary (September 2000)

**Roger M. Kubarych**
*Henry Kaufman Senior Fellow in International Economics and Finance*
Speaker

**Kenneth W. Dam**
*Max Pam Professor, American and Foreign Law, University of Chicago Law School*
Central Banking Group Chair

**Michael H. Moskow**
*President, Federal Reserve Bank of Chicago*
Economics & Trade Policy Group Chair

**John E. Rielly**
*President, Chicago Council on Foreign Relations*
Foreign Policy and National Security Group Chair

Tuesday, September 26, 2000
6:00–9:00 P.M.
The Chicago Council on Foreign Relations
Chicago, Illinois

# Participants

## Central Banking Group

A. Robert Abboud
*Robert Abboud and Company*

Tania Beil
*Chicago Council on Foreign
Relations*

Frederick C. Broda
*Oxford Analytica Inc.*

Marcia W. Dam
*United Nations High
Commissioner for Refugees*

John Fernald
*Federal Reserve Bank of Chicago*

Ronald Given
*Mayer, Brown & Platt*

David D. Hale
*Zurich Financial Services*

Alex J. Pollock
*Federal Home Loan Bank of
Chicago*

Edward Rouse
*Bain & Co.*

Leah Z. Wanger
*Liberty Wanger Asset
Management*

## Economics and Trade Policy Group

David Coolidge
*William Blair Capital
Management*

Bryant Garth
*American Bar Foundation*

Lyric M. Hughes
*China Online*

Paul Kasriel
*Northern Trust Company*

Richard T. Newman
*Lake Forest Capital
Management Co.*

Peter Pond
*Donaldson, Lufkin & Jenrette*

David J. Rosso
*Jones, Day, Reavis & Pogue*

Nathaniel Wuerffel
*Federal Reserve Bank of Chicago*

## Foreign Policy and National Security Group

Francis K. Bassolino
*University of Chicago*

Bartram S. Brown
*Chicago-Kent College of Law*

Joan Junkus
*DePaul University*

Edward A. Kolodziej
*University of Illinois*

Stephen Legg
*Haasard Productions*

Richard C. Longworth
*Chicago Tribune*

Harle G. Montgomery
*Kenneth F. and Harle G.*
*Montgomery Foundation*

James O'Shea
*Chicago Tribune*

Tammy Spath
*Chicago Council on Foreign*
*Relations*

David Webster
*A.T. Kearney, Inc.*

## Chicago Simulation Summary

Following the successful January 22, 2000, policy simulation in New York, we were encouraged to convene a second simulation in Chicago on September 26, 2000. This simulation, sponsored jointly by the Council on Foreign Relations and the Chicago Council on Foreign Relations, was based on the same scenario, "The Story So Far. . . ." However, the number of policy problems was pared back so that the exercise could fit into a two-hour time frame. To simplify the game further, we amalgamated the Central Banking and Financial Regulatory expert groups into a single Financial Policy Group. We also eliminated the distinction between policy recommendations and decisions by grafting the functions of the Decision-Makers Group into the Economics and Trade Policy Group and the Foreign Policy and National Security Group. But the content of each policy problem was essentially the same as in the New York simulation. The following gives a brief summary of the main policy decisions:

1. **U.S. Monetary Policy:** *What should be the appropriate cast of monetary policy during this period of U.S. financial market agitation?*
   The Financial Policy Group agreed that the troubled market situation required a loosening in the money supply in order to assure sufficient liquidity in the system. But there was considerable opposition to a massive easing in the stance of monetary policy because participants were intent on avoiding two potential dangers: reawakening inflation fears and precipitating a sharp decline in the value of the dollar in the foreign exchange markets.

If either of these dangers materialized, it would pose the threat of potential further selling of U.S. equities and fixed-income securities that would undercut the effort to stabilize the financial markets. Accordingly, the group decided on a ¼ percent reduction in the federal funds rate. The action would be taken without issuing a statement saying anything about what the central bank intended to do in the future, so as not to bias market expectations one way or the other. Meanwhile, the group favored establishment of a task force to address two issues: rising delinquencies among borrowers and possible problems within the payments system. The group also intended to work quietly with foreign central banks to deal with problems among individual financial institutions.

Discussion of further interest rate cuts was suspended when the group was informed that the Economics and Trade Policy Group had prepared a fiscal policy program that included substantial tax cuts [as described below].

2. **Saudi Arabia Foreign Policy Initiatives:** *Are the Saudi ambassador's talking points (in "The Story So Far...") for the White House briefing credible? Should the United States try to encourage or discourage the Saudis on any of the unprecedented courses of action described?*

The participants were divided on how seriously to take the Saudi ambassador's talking points. Some felt that they did not represent a credible package. Others felt that at least some elements deserved to be encouraged. They concluded that it was in the U.S. interest to urge the Saudis to go ahead with their proposed initiative to forge better relations with Iran. The participants thought that the Saudi hint to other Arab states to take steps to develop informal economic ties with Israel was a positive sign, and that the U.S. government needed to encourage the Israelis to pursue such indirect channels of communications. But there was complete skepticism that a similar bridge-building exercise with Iraq would make sense.

3. **Saudi Arabia Dollar Reserves:** *Should the United States consider accommodating the Saudi request for a special investment facility to*

*absorb the foreign exchange risk associated with their official dollar reserves?*

Members of the Financial Policy Group agreed that the United States should reject any such arrangement because of the bad precedent it would set and because it would inevitably encourage other countries to demand the same accommodation. The group felt that if the Saudis chose to diversify out of the dollar, this was their decision to make. Financial Policy Group participants were opposed to intervention in the foreign exchange markets and would be prepared to tolerate some depreciation of the dollar if that was how the market forces worked out. Members of the Economics and Trade Policy Group saw things differently. They were prepared to consider dollar-support actions if, as a quid pro quo, the Saudis would agree to produce a higher volume of oil.

4. **Ukraine-Russia Dispute:** *What is the significance for U.S.-Russian relations of Putin's hard-line stance toward Ukraine? What should the U.S. position be on any request for emergency financial assistance for Ukraine?*

The Foreign Policy and National Security Group concluded that the U.S. government should proceed by engaging with the Russian government to work cooperatively to help Ukraine overcome its serious economic and financial difficulties. Those problems require constructive thinking. The group resolved to tell the Russians that if they pushed Ukraine "to the wall" that they would be jeopardizing U.S. willingness to develop a closer relationship with Russia. Simultaneously, the group recommended that the U.S. government take steps to involve the leadership of the United Nations to help mediate negotiations between Ukraine and Russia toward resolving their disputes.

As for the immediate financial problems confronting the Ukrainian government, the Economics and Trade Policy Group were willing to consider extending a loan of up to $1 billion to help avert a debt default.

## 5. Turkey Plot Lines

a. **Banking crisis:** *How should the United States respond?*

Financial Policy Group members recommended that the U.S. government privately encourage Turkish authorities to take over responsibility of facilitating an orderly resolution of outstanding foreign currency contracts entered into by troubled Turkish banks. U.S. financial officials would then be expected to review carefully Turkish government actions to assure that implementation is effective. The Economics and Trade Policy Group agreed to this plan but went a step further, offering to provide financial assistance to maintain the stability of the payments system.

b. **IMF renegotiation:** *What should be the U.S. government policy toward a renegotiation of Turkey's IMF program?*

The Economics and Trade Policy Group decided that the U.S. government should support renegotiation and should use its influence to get the IMF to loosen conditions. The policy conditions originally agreed in December 1999 had turned out to be too ambitious and unrealizable in the short term. The group concluded that, while thoroughgoing policy reform was essential for Turkey's long-term economic and financial stability, it was important that the IMF impose only those conditions that could be implemented under difficult circumstances, so long as they began a process of moving the country's policies in the right direction.

c. **Human rights legislation/Incrlik access:** *How should the U.S. government handle the Incrlik issue and the question of how to respond to the proposed congressional legislation?*

The Foreign Policy and National Security Group agreed that it was important to keep Turkey in a friendly embrace. Among other things, that meant working to stop any legislation that would impose sanctions on Turkey. But members of the group agreed that it was worthwhile to use informal channels to impress on the Turks the need for them to improve their human rights record.

d. **Iran economic links:** *Under the Iran-Libya Sanctions Act (ILSA), should the U.S. government seek to apply sanctions against Turkish companies that have signed contracts with Iranian counterparts?*

The Foreign Policy and National Security Group did not support applying sanctions. It reasoned that Iran is softening up its policies toward the rest of the world. Foregoing the legal option could be viewed as an opportunity for the United States to encourage Iran to pursue a more liberal course.

e. **EU candidacy:** *How should the United States respond to the European Union's request to suspend support for Turkey joining the organization?*

In view of the significant gap between EU admission criteria and Turkey's economic performance, the Economics and Trade Policy Group agreed that the United States should refrain from putting public pressure on the European Union to accelerate Turkish membership.

6. **Argentina's Request for Financing Facility:** *How should the United States respond to this request? What are the foreign policy consequences if we do go along or do not go along with the Argentine request?*

The Foreign Policy and National Security Group recommended that the U.S. government go to the IMF to put together a new package of loans for Argentina, along the lines of the Mexican arrangements of 1995. If such support were not forthcoming, Argentina might be forced to default on its existing debt, an action that could destabilize the entire region— including Brazil. According to members of this group, the financial aid package should be conditioned on Argentina's acceptance of meaningful financial and economic reforms, including improvements in the Argentine government's budgetary policies. But this recommendation was overruled by the Central Banking and Economics and Trade Policy Groups. Their members were not convinced that such a program was desirable, either for the United States or for Argentina. They concluded that Argentina should let the peso float freely in the foreign currency markets rather than incur additional indebtedness to support a currency rate that might not be sustainable.

7. **U.S. Fiscal Policy Proposal:** After extensive discussion, the members of the Economics and Trade Policy Group concluded that the sharp contraction in the U.S. economy that was precipitated by the drop in the stock market required an activist fiscal policy approach. Accordingly, the participants agreed on a substantial 10 percent cut in marginal tax rates. They also proposed establishing an investment tax credit to promote a recovery in information technology (IT) capital expenditures by businesses operating in the United States.

8. **Libya-Russia:** *How should the United States respond to intelligence reports that Libya is developing a nuclear weapons capability based in large measure on imports of stolen nuclear material from Russia?*

The Foreign Policy and National Security Group agreed on a four-part strategy: first, initiating a diplomatic and economic response to hold Libya accountable and to press for a stop to its reported nuclear program; second, sending an emissary to Russia to gain its commitment to help stop the theft of nuclear materials and all shipments to Libya, offering whatever assistance the Russians might need to implement that effort; third, involving Israeli intelligence to verify U.S. intelligence sources and to develop an independent assessment of the alleged Libyan nuclear weapons program; and fourth, moving an aircraft carrier group into the area.

9. **Libya-Europe:** *How should the U.S. government respond to charges that Daimler-Chrysler and Airbus have entered into contracts with Libya that involve dual-use technology?*

The Economics and Trade Policy Group recommended making an example of the two companies by leaking to the press that the companies were under investigation for possible ILSA violations.

# *Appendix H*

# Roundtable on Lessons Learned and Policy Implications: List of Participants (November 2000)

November 10, 2000
12:15–2:00 P.M.

### Participants

Nicholas F. Beim
*Goldman, Sachs & Co.*

Sam Y. Cross
*Columbia University*

Craig Drill
*Craig Drill Capital*

William Flanagan
*Cantor Fitzgerald*

Leslie H. Gelb
*Council on Foreign Relations*

Richard K. Goeltz

Martin Gross
*Sandalwood Securities, Inc.*

David Kellogg
*Council on Foreign Relations*

Roger M. Kubarych
*Council on Foreign Relations*

Marc Levinson
*Chase Securities Inc.*

Michael P. Peters
*Council on Foreign Relations*

John J. Phelan Jr.

Cynthia A. Tindell
*Credit Suisse First Boston Corp.*

Laura Winthrop
*Council on Foreign Relations*

# Appendix I

# Washington, D.C., Conference Agenda (December 2000)

December 6, 2000
Council on Foreign Relations
Washington, D.C.


## Conference Program

8:00–8:30 A.M.    REGISTRATION AND CONTINENTAL BREAKFAST

8:30–9:00 A.M.    STRESS TESTING THE SYSTEM

**Roger M. Kubarych,** Henry Kaufman Senior Fellow in International Economics and Finance, Council on Foreign Relations

9:00–10:15 A.M.    HIGH-TECH VERSUS THE MARKET
*Is there a high-tech bubble? If so, how will its collapse affect the market?*

**Christopher C. Grisanti,** Principal, W.G. Spears Grisanti and Brown, LLC
**A. Alexander Porter Jr.,** General Partner, Porter Felleman, Inc.
**Michael Mandel,** Economics Editor, *Business Week*
*Moderator:* **Caren Bohan,** Correspondent, Reuters

10:15–10:30 A.M.   BREAK

10:30–12:00 P.M.  REGIONAL BREAKOUT SESSIONS:
WARNING SIGNS AND DAMAGE CONTROL
FINANCIAL, ECONOMIC, AND POLITICAL STRESS
TESTING

Participants will attend one of the three
Regional Breakout Sessions.

## 1. Asia

**Donald Gimbel,** Sr. Managing Director, Carret & Company
**Robert A. Manning,** C.V. Starr Senior Fellow and Director,
Asia Studies, Council on Foreign Relations
*Moderator:* **Richard T. McCormack,** former Under Secretary
of State for Economic and Business Affairs; International
Consultant

## 2. Europe and Russia

**Nicholas A. Rey,** Principal, Intellibridge Corporation
**Martin Walker,** Senior Fellow, Woodrow Wilson
International Center for Scholars
*Moderator:* **Ronald D. Asmus,** Senior Fellow, Europe
Studies, Council on Foreign Relations

## 3. Latin America

**David Roberts,** Sr. International Economist, Banc of
America Securities, LLC
**Mark Falcoff,** Resident Scholar, American Enterprise
Institute for Public Policy Research
*Moderator:* **Robert S. LaRussa,** Under Secretary for
International Trade, U.S. Department of Commerce

12:00–12:15 P.M  BREAK

12:15–1:45 P.M.  LUNCHEON
IMPROVING DECISION-MAKING IN AN
INCREASINGLY COMPLEX GLOBAL SYSTEM.

**Morris Goldstein,** Senior Fellow, Institute for
International Economics
**Nicholas Rostow,** International Lawyer;
former Staff Director, U.S. Senate Select

Committee on Intelligence
**Jeffrey Shafer,** Managing Director, Salomon
Smith Barney
*Moderator:* **Peter Gosselin,** Correspondent,
*Los Angeles Times*

1:45–2:00 P.M.    **BREAK**

2:00–2:30 P.M.    **REGIONAL BREAKOUT SESSION FINDINGS**
*Presented by group moderators*

2:30–3:45 P.M.    **DOWNSIDE SCENARIO: ANOTHER MARKET
BREAK? WHAT MIGHT BE THE ECONOMIC AND
POLITICAL BACKLASH?**
*Will Main Street stick with Wall Street in the
next financial crisis? Is the international spread
of an equity culture at risk?*

**Matthew P. Fink,** President, Investment
Company Institute
**Martin Mayer,** Guest Scholar, the Brookings
Institution
**Moderator: Laura S. Unger,** Commissioner,
Securities and Exchange Commission

3:45–4:00 P.M.    **BREAK**

4:00–5:15 P.M.    **NEW OPPORTUNITIES: LOOKING BEYOND NEAR-
TERM VULNERABILITIES: THE NEXT MARKET
DRIVERS**
*How will advances in emerging technologies
impact the economy and the financial markets?*

*Keynote Speaker:* **Wayne Knox,** Director of
Advanced Photonics Research, Bell Labs,
Lucent Technologies
*Moderator:* **Art Pine,** Columnist, Bloomberg
News

# About the Author

Roger M. Kubarych is the Henry Kaufman Adjunct Senior Fellow for International Economics and Finance and Director of International Economic Studies at the Council on Foreign Relations. Mr. Kubarych was the Managing Member and Chief Investment Officer of Kaufman & Kubarych Advisors, LLC (KKA), and was General Manager of Henry Kaufman & Company, Inc., from its inception in 1988 until KKA was established in January 1997.

Prior to joining Henry Kaufman & Company, Inc., Mr. Kubarych was Senior Vice President and Chief Economist of the New York Stock Exchange, where he directed the Economic Research Department from April 1986 to May 1988. From February 1985 to March 1986, he was Vice President and Chief Economist of the Conference Board, Inc., a business research organization.

Previously, Mr. Kubarych served thirteen years at the Federal Reserve Bank of New York in a variety of positions in the Research and Statistics Function and the Foreign Department. As Senior Vice President and Deputy Director of Research, he supervised research covering a wide range of economic and financial questions concerning the United States and foreign countries. During 1978 and 1979, he served as Special Assistant to the Under Secretary for Monetary Affairs at the U.S. Treasury.

He has published a number of papers and articles on economic and financial topics and is the author of *Foreign Exchange Markets in the United States*, now in its second edition and translated into Japanese. He frequently comments on financial markets and economic policy for such media organizations as CNN, Bloomberg, Nikkei, and NHK. He is a guest columnist for the German news weekly *Die Zeit*.

He is a graduate of Williams College, Oxford University, and Harvard University.